Ken Bernstein

J·P·M
PUBLICATIONS

# CONTENTS

# This Way Morocco

## Flight of Imagination

Some place-names incite dreams. Just to pronounce Katmandu or Mandalay can put a faraway look into a traveller's eyes. So it is with Marrakesh. Could the city really be as exotic, as engrossing, as unforgettable as its centuries-old reputation implies? You bet it could, even without the snake charmers and acrobats.

In Morocco all the cities seem to have evocative names. Think of Fez, Meknès and Tangier. In fact, you need hardly go beyond the nation's metropolis, Casablanca, to shift the imagination into high gear. Bogart is long gone, but it might as well be the 1940s in the hubbub of spice vendors, fish stalls and second-hand clothing merchants operating in the medina just around the corner from the new luxury hotels.

And consider the storied names of the country's most remarkable physical features: the Rif mountains, the Atlas mountains, and the Sahara desert. Even the map won't let you forget that this is no prosaic place.

## Coast to Coast

An ocean and a sea—the Atlantic and the Mediterranean—link Morocco to other continents, and incidentally provide refreshing breezes, outstanding beaches and memorable seafood dinners. With few exceptions, though, the "real" Morocco is inland: lonely mountain villages, cities built of mud, pervaded with medieval atmosphere, and the beauties and mysteries of the desert.

With an area of more than 710,000 sq km (nearly 275,000 sq miles), Morocco is bigger than Texas. (The official area includes disputed Saharan territories.) In a country that can grow tomatoes and dates at the same time, there is room enough for a great diversity in culture as well as climate. The California-style skyscrapers of Casablanca are a world away from the ochre kasbahs of the desert. Even within a single city, cultures collide. Donkeys go where taxis cannot pass, and a veiled traditionalist, hiding all her charms except the eyes, shops alongside young women in knee-length skirts.

The road signs are in Arabic and French. For historical reasons Spanish is the best-known foreign language of the north; elsewhere fluent French is heard. Among themselves the population speaks Arabic (the official language) and Berber (colloquially), depending on the region and the situation. Everyone drinks mint tea, most visibly the gregarious men of all ages, idling away so many hours in the cafés.

## A Glass of Tea

You may find yourself taking mint tea as the guest of a carpet merchant or a jewellery shop owner. The preparation, pouring and sipping of the refreshing beverage can be almost as meticulously mannered as the Japanese tea ceremony. Not only does the gesture reflect traditional Moroccan hospitality; it may also, by no coincidence, help persuade you to buy something.

If you hate haggling, try to make it a game—always a smile, always keeping in mind that the seller won't lose, no matter how fiercely you think you are bargaining. Just don't say "maybe" if you really mean "no".

Shopping in Morocco starts with morocco—the fine, soft leather that has taken the country's name for centuries, as in morocco-bound books. Less celebrated leather turns up in every souk in every form from suitcases to camel saddles. After you've bought a pair of slippers, you may want to go all the way and acquire a kaftan or a jellaba. As well as necklaces, copper and brassware—and the carpet that caught your eye at the outset.

## The Choices

Morocco can be as strenuous as you want to make it. Mount a camel—a one-humped dromedary, to be exact—to have your picture taken, or lope off for a week-long Sahara safari from oasis to oasis. Admire the Atlas mountains from a palm grove in the desert, or climb Mount Toubkal, at 4,167 m (13,672 ft) the highest peak in North Africa. Lounge on a beach or build some muscles fighting the waves and the breeze on a sailboard.

On land or sea, the sporting possibilities are extravagant. You can water-ski in the Mediterranean or ski down the snowy

**1** **THE BEST MOSQUE** Until modern times the immense, ancient Karaouine Mosque in Fez was the largest in Morocco. Now it has been overtaken by Casablanca's **King Hassan II Mosque**, a colossal statement of faith rising just above the Atlantic waves. Laser lighting effects crown its minaret, visible for miles around, with a sort of celestial cloud.

*Fishing boats ply the River Bou Regreg alongside national capital, Rabat.*

slopes only an hour away from the poolside in Marrakesh. Trout fishermen go to the rivers, bass and perch anglers take to Morocco's lakes, and for everything up to shark and blue fin tuna, the ocean awaits. Golf and polo fit for a king and tennis galore keep landlubber sportsmen out of mischief.

## After Sunset

When the breeze begins to rustle the palm fronds and the muezzin chants his call to early evening prayer, it's time to abandon the swimming pool and think about the hours ahead. Moroccans, 99 per cent of them Muslims, tend to avoid alcohol, but they are tolerant of the tastes of strangers, so the hotel barmen can mix up any cocktail you may fancy. Wine is produced more than competently in Morocco, and you'll have no problem finding a suitable vintage to accompany your dinner. The national cuisine ranges from homely, spicy standbys to the most exquisite delicacies.

After dinner you may want to investigate the music of the country and study the applied art of belly dancing, or work off your own calories in the hotel's disco. Whatever your choice, it's a perfect contrast to the day's adventures.

5

# *Flashback*

## Scenes from History

In the beginning the Sahara was nothing like the ocean of sand that awes us today. Until only a few thousand years ago it was fertile enough to support the kind of animals featured in southern African safaris, from elephants to zebras. When it all dried up, primitive farmers turned into nomads, among them the first Moroccans. In some ways the Berbers are about as mysterious now as they ever were. They speak hundreds of local dialects throughout Africa, and, though fiercely independent, they have never formed a nation of their own.

## The Phoenician Connection

Recorded history starts around 1000 BC when Phoenician traders opened a branch office at what is now the enclave of Melilla, on the Mediterranean coast. The Carthaginians, who eventually took over the Phoenician business, expanded commercial operations as far as Lixus (Larache), on the Atlantic. Cartha-ginian inscriptions have been unearthed inland, too, at Volubilis, near Meknès. After winning the Punic Wars, the Roman empire brutally erased Carthage from the map in 146 BC, though the word didn't reach far-flung colonies for years.

## Mauretania Tingitana

The Romans developed North Africa as their bread basket. Eager administrators, they split it into four provinces; Morocco and Algeria were combined as *Mauretania Tingitana*—named after Tingis, now Tangier. Tingis won the rank of full-scale Roman city in 38 BC. One name shines from the archives of that epoch. The handsome, intellectual King Juba II of Mauretania, a Berber by birth, won the hand of Cleopatra Selene, thus becoming the son-in-law of Antony and Cleopatra. Alas, the saga ended unhappily. Around AD 40 the son of Juba and Cleo, Ptolemy, made a bad impression on the moody emperor Caligula, who ordered the lad executed.

## Christians and Jews

The Romans had a hard time pacifying the Berbers and never ventured very far south, with

*Rabat's Hassan minaret looms over ruins of the vast 12th-century mosque.*

Rabat their farthest-flung settlement. From Rome, Christianity spread through the empire, and by the 3rd century Morocco had four bishoprics. (There was also a significant Jewish culture, the result of migrations after the fall of Jerusalem in AD 70. The Jewish traditions, often combined with Berber customs, have been part of the Moroccan scene into modern times.) But the Roman empire was in free-fall decline and Morocco suffered the fringe of the Vandal unpleasantness that afflicted the Europe of the Dark Ages, in addition to wars, insurrections and all-around confusion.

### The Islamic Tide

Early in the 7th century in the Arabian city of Mecca, the Prophet, Mohammed, heard a divine message and set it down in the Koran. Within a century of Mohammed's death in 632, the new religion had raced across Arabia and conquered hearts and minds all over the Middle East and North Africa.

Despatched from Damascus, the first Arab invaders sliced into Morocco in 682. They were led by Uqba Ibn Nafi, a dauntless general who went as far as he could go—overland to the Atlantic ocean at Agadir. Although he took key hostages to encourage the Berber tribes to convert, the

Islamization of Morocco wasn't as quick and spontaneous as he might have hoped.

### Into Spain

Northern Morocco, under Arab control early in the 8th century, was the embarkation point for the Moorish invasion of Europe. Tough Berber troops, newly converted to Islam, spearheaded the amphibious attack on Gibraltar in 711. Spain turned out to be a walkover for the invaders, who within a few years had conquered almost all the territory up to the Pyrenees. The capital of Muslim-occupied Spain, established in Córdoba, became one of the world's biggest, most beautiful and refined cities.

The Reconquest of Spain by the Christian forces seesawed for nearly eight centuries.

### The First Dynasty

Back in Morocco, a great-grandson of the Prophet arrived towards the end of the 8th century to inspire the faithful and set the stage for an Arab kingdom. Moulay Idris reigned but briefly from the old Roman city of Volubilis before he was assassinated, poisoned; his memory is revered in the nearby hill town named after him. The dynasty he founded, the Idrisids, went on to considerable achievements. His heir, Idris II, a posthumous child by a Berber mother, set up his capital at Fez. The city's greatness was soon spurred by the arrival of devout, skilled workers from Córdoba and Tunisia's religious centre, Kairouan. You could say that Idris I and II were the founding fathers of Morocco.

## The Almoravids

It lasted less than a century, but the Almoravid dynasty unified the country and spread Morocco's power as far as Algiers and Andalusia. The Almoravids were nomadic Berbers from the desert of what is now Mauritania, as ascetic and devout as the toughest, most puritanical warrior-monks. They forced their standards on the people and built a fortress at Marrakesh. As time passed, the Almoravids were softened by the civilization that surrounded them, as well as the influence of the Spanish branch of the family. Art began to flourish in Morocco, and one of the most magnificent mosques in all Islam, the Karaouine mosque, brought splendour to Fez. On the military front, Emir Yusuf ibn Tashfin took up the struggle for Islam in Spain and won a crucial victory over King Alfonso VI of Castile in 1086.

## The Almohads

Early in the 12th century another Berber dynasty, the fervent Almohads, took power and quickly propelled Morocco to imperial greatness. Before their era waned, nearly 150 years later, they ruled over all of North Africa and much of southern Spain. An Almohad sultan, Yacoub el Mansour, won a big battle in Spain in 1195, then devoted himself to embellishing his reign. He built a new capital in Rabat and sponsored the exquisite minarets of Marrakesh and Seville.

In science, engineering, architecture, art and all-round culture the Almohads presided over the most brilliant chapter of the golden age.

## Setbacks

The Merinid dynasty, headquartered in a flourishing Fez, continued the cultural and artistic achievements of the Almohads while suffering battlefield reverses. Among their greatest successes was building the fabulous Alhambra complex in Granada, but soon only Granada kept the faith in a Spain all but recaptured by the Christians. As if the Spanish situation wasn't difficult enough, the Portuguese began raids on the Moroccan coast. Less than 30 years after the Merinids had been ousted, Granada, too, finally surrendered—to the "Catholic monarchs", Ferdinand and Isabella. 9

Muslims and Jews expelled from the Spain of the Inquisition rushed to asylum in Morocco.

## The Saadians

The Saadian dynasty reversed a trend of military setbacks in the 16th century, ousting the Portuguese from some, though not all, of their Moroccan footholds. The wily, expansionist Ahmad al-Mansur won glory by capturing Timbuktu and bringing back slaves and gold.

Under the Saadians, corsairs ran a profitable privateering industry from Moroccan ports, part of the lurid era of the Barbary (from "Berber") pirates.

## Moulay Ismaïl

A larger than life sultan, Moulay Ismail, who reigned as a very effective tyrant from 1672 to 1727, chalked up many successes in military and diplomatic affairs. He ousted European expansionists from most of their Moroccan beachheads and kept the Turks at bay. His greatest monument is the palatial city of Meknès, where he is buried. The far-sighted Moulay Ismaïl was an early monarch of the Alaouite dynasty, which claimed descent from the Prophet.

Through thick and thin the dynasty has shown exceptional longevity; the incumbent King Hassan II is the latest of the line.

## 'Protectorate'

French, Spanish and to a lesser degree German interests became ever more forceful early in the 20th century. After their initial economic penetration the Europeans began nibbling away territory—France took Casablanca, Spain occupied historic Ksar el Kabir, south of Tangier. (Spain had held enclaves on the north coast for centuries: Melilla and Ceuta are still Spanish External Provinces.)

In 1912 an economically vulnerable Morocco agreed to the Treaty of Fez establishing a Franco-Spanish "protectorate". When Berbers in the Rif mountains rebelled in the 1920s, France and Spain sent in hundreds of thousands of troops to restore control.

## Towards Independence

Demands for Moroccan independence, coordinated by the new Istiqlal party, surfaced during World War II. The sultan, Mohammed V, sympathized, at first silently, and then with words and actions, and finally the French lost patience. The sultan was deposed in 1953, exiled to Madagascar. By the time he returned triumphantly to Morocco two years later, the struggle had almost been won.

Independence was signed and sealed in 1956, and Mohammed

V ruled as a popular king until his tragic death after a minor operation in 1961.

## A New Reign

By the time Hassan II assumed the throne, his whole life had been a training course for the political and religious leadership of his country. As crown prince he had been doubly educated, in Arabic and French. His reign would survive economic strains, political unrest, a failed coup and an assassination attempt.

## Frontiers of the Future

Morocco's territory was greatly enlarged in 1976 after the dramatic Green March of thousands of citizens to the western Sahara. The ultimate details of the disputed borders are to be decided by a UN-run referendum. Meanwhile, Morocco is developing the mineral-rich territory whose capital, Laayoune, has bloomed.

The king's most spectacular monument, the Hassan II mosque on the seafront in Casablanca, was consecrated in 1993.

11

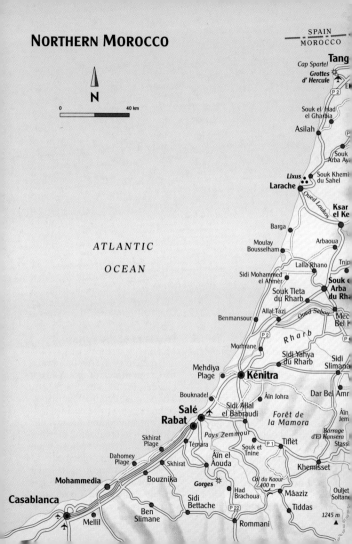

# NORTHERN MOROCCO

N

0          40 km

*ATLANTIC*

*OCEAN*

SPAIN
MOROCCO

**Tang**
Cap Spartel
Grottes
d' Hercule
P 2

Souk el Had
el Gharbia

Asilah

Souk
Arba Aya

*Lixus*                Souk Khemi
**Larache**         du Sahel

Oued Loukos

**Ksar
el Ke**

Barga

Arbaoua

Moulay
Bousselham

Lalla Rhano              Tnip

Sidi Mohammed
el Ahmer

Souk Tleta                  **Souk e
du Rharb**                  **Arba
du Rha**

Allal Tazi

Benmansour              Oued Sebou        **Mec
Bel H**

P 2                          P

*Rharb*

Morhrane

Sidi Yahya          **Sidi
du Rharb**          **Slimana**

Mehdiya
Plage          **Kénitra**

Bouknadel                Aïn Johra        Dar Bel Amr

**Salé**          Sidi Allal
**Rabat**          el Babraudi          *Forêt de*          Aïn
                                        *la Mamora*          Jem

Skhirat                                              *Barrage*
Plage                                              *d'El Kansera*
Témara          Souk et          P 1          Stassi
Dahomey          Tnine          Tiflèt
Plage          Skhirat
                Aïn el
**Mohammedia**          *Aouda*
                *Gorges*          Col du Kaour          Khemisset
**Casablanca**          Bouznika          Had          400 m                Oujlet
                              Brachoua                              Soltane
        Mellil          Sidi          P 22          Mâaziz
                Bettache                          Tiddas
        Ben
        Slimane          Rommani          1245 m

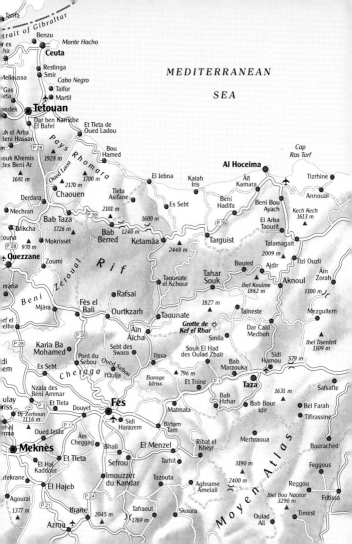

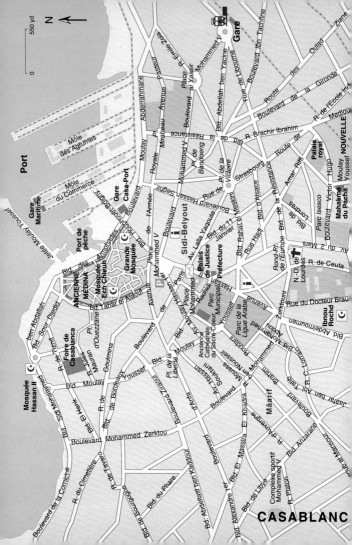

# On the Scene

*The most popular sightseeing itineraries start with the imperial cities. Other programmes go logically from north to south, from the Mediterranean shore to the deepest Sahara. And some sun-lovers never get beyond the beach at Agadir. This guide divides the essentials into half a dozen sectors, starting with the country's first and second largest cities—the capitals of industry and politics, less than 100 km (62 miles) apart, and ending with a section on the desert and oases.*

## CAPITALS

Casablanca, Rabat, Salé

The cities are so close together that they share the same international airport. Going from the centre of Casablanca to the centre of Rabat takes less than an hour on the comfortable commuter train, a bit more on the motorway. These utterly different cities make a fine match: "Casa" for its enthusiasm and commercial power, Rabat for history, space and grace.

### Casablanca

About one in ten of all Moroccans lives in Casablanca. Almost everything dates from the 20th century, most winningly in the newest areas of the city centre, shining with contemporary architecture and comfortable wealth. Palm trees eight storeys tall line the boulevards, which are interspersed with shady parks containing outdoor cafés and ice-cream shops.

### Hassan II Mosque

You can't miss the "new beacon of Islam" on the Atlantic shore of Casablanca, the Hassan II Mosque. The country's tallest structure, the minaret is nearly 200 m (655 ft) high. It dominates the skyline from land and sea, day and (especially) night, when it is dramatically lit and the laser beam on top illuminates the way to Mecca. The Mega-Mosque, as it has been nicknamed, is the biggest anywhere outside of Mecca: the prayer hall is the size of four football fields, and an overflow crowd of 80,000 additional faithful can easily be accommodated on the esplanade outside. All the auxiliary facilities, from *medersa* (religious school) to underground garages, are on a similar superlative scale. The architect, Michel Pinseau, is French; thousands of Moroccan artisans produced the impressive details of a monument that imposes spirituality on the bustling commercial city.

### Colonial City

When the French landed in Casablanca in 1907 the population was scarcely 20,000. The spacious colonial city they built is criss-crossed by stately boulevards and centred on the square called Place des Nations Unies. A grand municipal ensemble combines European and Moorish architectural elements in a style referred to as Mauresque. The planners couldn't resist crowning the arcaded city hall with the sort of clock tower that would be more suitable on a railway station.

An attractive vestige of the colonial era, the Sacred Heart Cathedral (*Cathédrale du Sacré Cœur*) has been deconsecrated, but its uplifting design adds to Casablanca's attractions. Several smaller churches still serve the local Christian community.

### Old Medina

Once you're inside the old walled city, it's self-explanatory. The medina is small enough to ensure that you don't get seriously lost, the streets are relatively wide and bright, the salesmen on the whole no more grasping than a friendly shoal of octopuses. If you're not in the market for a second-hand watch or a slightly used radio, browse among the alluring food stalls.

### To the Beach

The other side of big-city life is out beyond the port, the old medina and the titanic new mosque, in the suburb of Aïn Diab. The corniche road leads to a string of luxurious hotels, clubs and resorts on the ocean. This is where Casablanca people go in summer

16

*Hassan II Mosque crowns the skyline of modern, high-rise Casablanca.*

to escape the heat, eat seafood, have a swim (probably in a sea-water pool) and meet friends.

Tricky tides grip the Atlantic here, and the water is hardly clean and pure, but Aïn Diab is worth a look, and a breath of sea air.

## Rabat

The French can take credit for transforming it into a worthy capital, but Rabat, sited where the Bou Regreg River meets the Atlantic, has been a significant city since the time of the Romans. The most remarkable monuments on view today reflect achievements from early medie-val times to the present reign. One of the most striking juxtapositions anywhere is the 12th-century Hassan Tower next door to the 1970s mausoleum of Mohammed V.

### The Medina

This is surely the medina for beginners. Unlike the mazes of some other cities, Rabat's old town follows a grid pattern of straight streets where it's fairly difficult to lose your way. Another advantage: the merchants are so low-key they wouldn't hassle a fly. But there's no shortage of local colour. Just inside the gate, public scribes with type-

17

writers fill in forms for illiterate or unsure clients. Here, too, lurk artisans in hope of work—house-painters with their rollers and brushes, masons with their trowels. The supply far exceeds the demand. There are beggars with every imaginable disability, and some you could never have imagined.

The shopping includes silk embroidery, jewellery, brightly coloured Rabat carpets, copperware, and leather.

### Kasbah des Oudaïas

Just north (and uphill) from the medina, the lived-in kasbah is an atmospheric zone in which to wander, but be wary of would-be guides who don't hesitate to point non-clients in a wrong direction.

The main entrance to the enclave is through Bab al-Kasbah, otherwise called the Oudaïa gate, a glorious example of decorative stonecarving from the end of the 12th century. The kasbah's main street leads past iron-studded house doors and the oldest mosque in Rabat to the open cannon-and-semaphore platform, with views over the ocean, the river and the town of Salé on the opposite bank.

Another vantage point nearby is a shaded outdoor café in a cool and restful Andalusian-style garden. A stairway climbs from here to a restored 17th-century palace, which houses the Museum of Moroccan Arts. It features all national crafts from polychrome pottery and Berber jewellery to local carpets.

### The Mausoleum

Mounted soldiers in theatrical red uniforms maintain a vigil at the entrance to the complex containing the tomb of Mohammed V, father of the present king, and the adjacent ruins of a mosque from the Almohad era. The mausoleum itself is protected by a guard of honour of dismounted troops; the changing of the guard is not quite in the Buckingham Palace precision league but definitely worth a picture.

All the traditional Moroccan arts and materials are utilized in the modern mausoleum—tile, marble, precious stones and brass worked to perfection. Unusually, non-Muslims are permitted inside, to look down on the white onyx sarcophagus.

### Hassan Tower

The Hassan Mosque was an ambitious 12th-century project, abandoned on the death of the expansionist sultan Yacoub el Mansour. The size of the mosque is apparent from the forest of stumps of columns arrayed here. What's left standing tall is one of the most beautiful minarets anywhere. The Hassan Tower dates 19 from the same time and inspiration as Seville's Giralda and the Koutoubia minaret in Marrakesh.

### Archaeological Museum

Cats and kittens cavort playfully in the patio of the Archaeological Museum, in the new town. The main exhibition covers a bit of everything ancient, from the most primitive stones of prehistoric times to oil lamps, jewellery and coins, and early Islamic-era pottery. But the museum's most valuable possessions are kept in the annexe, labelled the Bronze Collection. The star attraction is a beautiful sculpture showing the Berber features of King Juba II, excavated at Volubilis.

### Chellah

The necropolis of the Merinid dynasty, a fortress called the Chellah, was built in the 14th century on the site of the Roman colony of Sala. Ruins of a Roman forum, a temple, shops and baths have been unearthed within the walls. Notwithstanding the scattering of royal tombs and a roofless mosque with a crumbled minaret, the Chellah is a most cheerful place to visit. A lovely tropical garden makes all the difference.

### Salé

Named after the Roman Sala, the walled city of Salé was founded in the 11th century. You can get there by bus, grand-taxi or rowing boat. In the Middle Ages, sailboats reached the town along a long-lost channel reaching the giant gate called Bab el Mrisa. Religious monuments are the main "official" sights—the Almohad grand mosque (the interior is off limits to non-Muslims) and the spacious Merinid-era medersa, decorated with ceramic tiles and carved screens. "Unofficially", the medina, unspoiled, is off the tourist track and the souks are thoroughly colourful.

**2 THE TWO BEST ROMAN RUINS** The Romans colonized as far afield as Rabat, but the most impressive ruins are **Volubilis,** near Meknès, and **Lixus,** near Larache. The Volubilis site, dominating a magnificent plateau, is so big that coach loads of tourists don't impinge on each other. The Lixus ruins evoke the legends of Hercules and civilizations of Carthage as well as Rome.

# NORTH COAST

Tangier, Tetouan, Chaouen, Asilah, Lixus

It's only 13 km (8 miles) from Tangier to Spain, so close you can almost hear the wail of a flamenco singer wafting across the Strait of Gibraltar. At the crossroads of the Atlantic and the Mediterranean, this northern coast of Morocco has a chequered history and a cosmopolitan appeal.

## Tangier

International intrigue, smugglers, refugees, eccentric or disreputable characters—the tolerant people of Tangier, who cheerfully call themselves Tangerines,

have seen it all. Three thousand years ago the Phoenicians set up a trading post and fishing port here. Later it became the Roman town of Tingis. Arab rulers arrived in the 8th century, and Portugal captured the city in the 15th. For a time it belonged to Charles II of England. In 1906 the city came under the control of eight European powers while Spain ruled the rest of the North. Which is why your school Spanish will take you far in Tangier and northern Morocco.

### Grand Socco

Just outside the old town walls, the Grand Socco—the big souk— is one of the traditional centres of Tangier life. From here you walk through an archway into the medina, a bustling hillside of winding streets and lanes in which artisans of different trades —woodworkers, jewellers, shoemakers—congregate.

### Petit Socco

In the heart of the medina, the Petit Socco (the little souk) is a pleasant open space with several cafés. It used to be a crossroads of intrigue in the Gateway to Africa. All Tangier still passes here—businessmen in striped

---

**SHUN THE HUSTLERS**

Most tourist areas in Morocco are afflicted with unofficial guides, freelance shopping advisers, confidence tricksters and aggressive hawkers. As the first stop for many visitors, Tangier is perhaps the national capital of hustlers; they seem to speak a little of every language on earth, and they aim to separate you from some—if not all—of your money. Learning how to say "no" with a smile is part of your education. If you need a genuine guide, go to the tourist office.

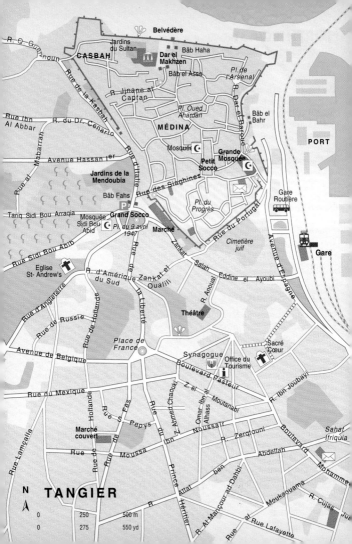

jellabas, women in kaftans or Paris dresses, and a mischievous cast of children.

## Kasbah

At the top of the hill above the medina, the kasbah seems impregnable from land or sea. This fortress was the centre of administration of old Tangier, where Moulay Ismail chose to build his palace behind the batteries of cannon installed on the walls. The Sultan's Garden, part of Moulay Ismail's 17th-century palace, is just beyond a large unmarked doorway in Rue Riad Sultan. From the fragrant garden you enter the sultan's palace, Dar el Makhzen.

## Museum of Moroccan Arts

The palace's Museum of Moroccan Arts covers all manner of treasures, from illuminated Korans to wood and metal work, as well as Berber carpets and a collection of ceramics. The adjoining Antiquities Museum goes back as far as Stone Age finds and Roman mosaics. With its two richly decorated courtyards, the palace itself is a work of art.

## Forbes Museum

The unconventional American magazine publisher Malcolm Forbes, remembered for his motorcycle-riding and party-giving, maintained a residence in the Mendoub Palace in Rue Shakespeare. He died in 1990 and left a record-breaking collection of toy soldiers, many deployed to illustrate notable battles, in the Forbes Museum of Military Miniatures.

## New Town

Leading south from the Grand Socco, the Rue de la Liberté goes to the heart of the modern city of Tangier—Place de France and Boulevard Pasteur. Cafés, restaurants, travel agencies and bookstores are all within a few streets, and there's a fine panorama of the harbour and the Spanish mainland from the terrace.

## Cap Spartel

A few miles due west of Tangier, an old lighthouse stares out at all the supertankers sailing between the Atlantic and the Mediterranean. You can climb the spiral staircase to the observation level and celebrate the superlative: Cap Spartel is the northwesternmost point in Africa. Robinson beach is an inviting, endless expanse of sand but the tides make it risky for swimmers. Down the coast, prehistoric people quarried stone in the Caves of Hercules. The mythological hero Hercules, or Heracles, is a household name hereabouts, for his labours were said to have created the Strait of Gibraltar.

23

## ENCLAVES

Since the 15th and 16th centuries, two Spanish possessions have been clinging to the northern coast of Morocco. Ceuta and Melilla both have Spanish military bases, *paradores*, brandy and sherry for sale, *paella* on the menu and, in Melilla, a bull ring. Morocco periodically asks for the return of the territory, ironically a mirror image of Spain's claims on Gibraltar across the way. Tensions are well under control.

## Tetouan

Echoes of Andalusia account for the charm of Tetouan, a skyline of whitewashed houses on the slopes of the Rif mountains overlooking the Mediterranean. The city traces its history back more than 2,000 years, but the modern phase began at the end of the 15th century when Muslim and Jewish refugees from the Christian Reconquest of Spain flooded in. They brought with them the skills of Andalusian architects, artists and artisans.

### Place Hassan II

The thoroughly modern ceremonial square of Tetouan is a wide open space bordered by palm trees, flag-poles and tiled minaret-like towers; the paving interweaves geometric forms. It's all a startling departure from the typical traditional Moroccan square. A newly restored Royal Palace occupies one end.

### The Medina

Fine Andalusian touches such as wrought-iron balconies and colourful tile decorations make this the ultimate Mauresque medina of Morocco. In the souks, Tetouan's shopping temptations, from textiles to pottery to contraband from the nearby Spanish enclave of Ceuta, ambush the visitor at every turning.

## Chaouen

Red-tile roofs and whitewashed walls distinguish the small mountain town of Chaouen, also known as Chefchaouen or Xauen, founded in the 15th century. Isolated for hundreds of years, the inhabitants maintained their Andalusian architecture, gardens and handicrafts. There are two main squares: Place Outa el Hammam, next to the kasbah, and the more formal, fountained Place El Makhzen. Plunge into Chaouen's souks and immerse yourself in the animation, the sounds and aromas of this singular town.

## Asilah

An hour's drive down the Atlantic coast from Tangier, the fishing port of Asilah has a dis-

*Rifles ablaze (firing blanks), fantasia horsemen gallop at a festival.*

tinctive sort of charm, celebrated only in recent years with the inauguration of an international cultural festival. Asilah has been around since Phoenician days but the dominant influence visible today comes from the Portuguese, who fortified the town in the 15th and 16th centuries. The roomy but labyrinthine streets of the medina are easily explored, with ramparts and towers as reminders of the days of derring-do. In the early 20th century a notorious brigand named Raisuli had a palace built overlooking the sea. It figures in the international festival in August. Other attractions are a long beach and some relaxed seafood restaurants whose reputation spreads as far as Tangier.

## Lixus

Just north of the quiet port of Larache, Lixus was an important colony of ancient Rome, with much evidence to prove it. On the site you can inspect the remains of an acropolis, temples, an amphitheatre, and in the lower town, salt and fish-sauce factories. Legend places the Garden of Hesperides alongside the river Loukos at Lixus. Here Hercules would have stolen golden apples as the penultimate challenge on his way to Mount Olympus.

25

# IMPERIAL HEART
### Meknès, Moulay Idris, Volubilis, Fez

In the strategic central area of Morocco, two imperial capitals within 60 km (less than 40 miles) of each other but hundreds of years apart vie for sumptuous extremes. Excursions nearby unearth the glory that was Rome and the mystique of an Islamic saint. To the south, the Middle Atlas hints at the dizzying mountain experience that awaits.

## Meknès
The Alaouite Sultan Moulay Ismaïl, who ruled from 1672 to 1727, has been called the Louis XIV of Morocco. If that means thinking big in the pursuit of glory, it's easy to see the link between the two contemporaries. For Louis, Versailles was the ultimate extravagance. For the ruthless Moulay Ismaïl, look no farther than his capital of Meknès, full of grandiose projects begun in his reign. Some are in ruins but enough are preserved to testify to a magnificent dream. Starting with a gateway of remarkable power and beauty.

### Bab Mansour
The city walls of Meknès stretch for perhaps 25 km (15 miles), interspersed with gates that are ceremonial or fortress-style or utilitarian. The most wondrous of all is the monumental Bab Mansour, named after the architect, a Christian slave converted to Islam. The symmetry of the enormous ensemble warms the spirit. Take the time to absorb the intricacies of the decorations above the main horseshoe arch and the smaller side arches for the bastions. (Among the inscriptions in graceful calligraphy are mighty praise for Moulay Ismaïl and his son, Moulay Abdallah, who finished the job.)

### Mausoleum
Moulay Ismaïl enlisted everybody available to build his city—artisans, labourers, tribesmen and slaves. In his relentless and comprehensive construction programme, he didn't forget to build his own last resting place. Pilgrims, especially country folk, still come to the lavish mausoleum to pray in the memorial mosque. The unpredictable sultan was reputed to have crowds of victims on his conscience, but because of his religious fervour he is still seen as saintly. Exceptionally, non-Muslims are permitted to peer into, but not quite set foot in, the mosque of the Moulay Ismaïl Mausoleum.

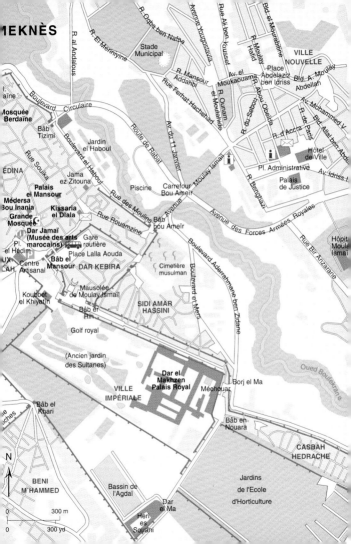

*The Roman empire's farthest-flung outpost: Volubilis, near Meknès.*

### Dar Jamaï

A highlight of the medina, Dar Jamaï is a 19th-century palace now serving as a museum of Moroccan arts. A minister of the sultan's court lived in this palace in an enviable state of luxury. Among the works of art and handicrafts on display are carpets from the Middle Atlas mountains, household furnishings, embroidery, decorative wall tiles, pottery and jewellery. The palace itself remains a delight to the eye.

### The Souks

Just around the corner from the museum-palace begin the souks, where artisans produce every-

thing from carpet slippers to saddles, from wedding gowns to tea pots. You can see a carpet woven, a table sanded, a fancy kaftan sewn. All the fragrances of the orient are here, from the saffron on sale in giant sacks to the skewered meat sizzling on the grill. Here, too, you can purchase herbs and traditional health foods, including plump, live lizards whose blood is said to be a reliable tonic.

### Bou Inania Medersa

This 14th-century religious college surrounds a tiled courtyard equipped with a tinkling marble fountain for meditative background music. It was built about the same time as a medersa of the same name, a landmark of Fez. Outstanding here is the wood-work—the complex carving of cedar screens enclosing the dormitory.

You can visit the student cells, then climb to the roof for a view of the Grand Mosque next door, with its red-tiled roofs and green-tiled minaret.

## Moulay Idris

Pilgrims have climbed the hill-sides of this white-walled town north of Meknès for centuries. Here is the tomb of a great-grand-son of the Prophet Mohammed, the sultan-saint Moulay Idris, founder of the first Moroccan Arab dynasty. Non-Muslims are forbidden to enter the shrine and adjacent *zaouia,* but the rest of the town is open to infidels, if not necessarily warmly welcoming. The town of Moulay Idris looks inward with a self-sufficient air. You can mount the zigzag streets for a look down onto the green tile roofs of the monuments and the countryside of olive trees, pines and cactus.

## Volubilis

They came a long way, but the ancient Romans found a majestic site for their farthest-flung Afri-can city. The Phoenicians seem to have been here several centu-ries earlier but by the first century AD this was a key outpost of the Roman province of Mauretania Tingitana.

Volubilis looks out on moun-tains and valleys to inspire a poet—a 360-degree view of the best of North African scenery. New colonists arriving here at the end of an incredible overland voyage from the Mediterranean must have been cheered at the familiar sight of cedar trees and a ceremonial arch. Today it's an easy half-day-trip from Meknès, a chance to wander through acres of evocative ruins.

### On Site

For a modest admission fee you can follow the path across a negligible ravine and up to the heart of the archaeological site. Few signs inform the visitor, but it's hard to get lost. And should you happen to enter somewhere out of bounds or climb on to deli-cate stonework a guardian will blow a police whistle to restore order.

Among the first sights is a Roman olive oil factory and storage facility. The region is still in the olive business, and the tech-nical side hasn't changed a lot. Nearby, the foundations of the luxurious House of Orpheus show the sophistication of the plumb-ing and heating; fine mosaics are preserved.

29

## The Forum

At the top of the town, the Forum was the centre of life in Volubilis. Here is the Basilica, with many arches still standing, and the columned Capitol. The Triumphal Arch, incompletely restored but obviously a stately landmark, was dedicated to the Emperor Caracalla. Between the arch and the Tangier Gate runs the main street, Decumanus Maximus, lined by the remains of aristocratic houses and palaces. Some classic mosaics remain where they were unearthed, but many valuable artefacts and statues wound up in museums or farther afield.

## Fez

Famous for their self-assurance and sophistication, the people of Fez don't hide their pride in the city, which has been a political, spiritual, intellectual and commercial centre for centuries. Fez can be a jolt for outsiders, mixing the most memorable contrasts: splendours of classical art, the down-to-earth bustle of everyday life, and the stench of medieval industry. Watch your step.

*Colourful Fez: ancient dyeing vats are still in use in the souk; a picturesque crowd passes through one of the monumental gateways.*

## TANNERS AND DYERS

The most fragrant place to be in the Fez medina is the spice market, where the aromas of mint, saffron and dozens of other scents compete for your pleasure. Less alluring is the smell of cloth drying in the dyers' souk, though the colours are wonderful. Worst of all is the heavy stench pervading the tanneries, where fresh animal hides are cleaned and shaped, then tanned and dried in hellish heat. The process has hardly changed since the Middle Ages.

### Claims to Greatness

Fez can trace its history to the era of Moulay Idris, the 8th century "patron saint". His son, Idris II, continued the work, building a royal palace, a market and town walls, and welcoming talented immigrants from Andalusia. Devout refugees from a Berber pogrom in Kairouan (Tunisia) founded the Karaouine Mosque. This 9th-century institution included what is now the world's oldest existing university. (Europe's oldest university, at Bologna, wasn't established until the 11th century.) Later dynasties embellished old Fez with fortifications, schools, mosques and shrines. Morocco's first imperial city, Fez stood unchallenged astride the trade routes linking the Sahara and the Mediterranean.

### Fes el Bali

The oldest part of Fez, very much a lived-in part of the city, is overpoweringly exotic. You'll want to see Fes el Bali's formal historical monuments, but what will linger longest in your memory is the experience of mingling with ordinary people going about their business in a timeless swirl of outlandish sights and smells. Donkeys are the taxis of the medina, but there are traffic jams in the narrow lanes, and it gets messy underfoot. (Listen for the cry *"balek!"*, warning that traffic is directly behind you.) Each craft congregates in its own mini-neighbourhood—tailors squatting in adjacent open shop-fronts, needles flashing as they stitch a metre a minute; nearby the fragrance of cedar shavings advertises the realm of the carpenters. In the closed world of the medina, the sawdust doesn't go to waste—it fuels the fire that heats the water in the nearby *hammam*, the communal baths.

### Bab Boujeloud

The most beautiful way in to the medina is through a celebrated gate, Bab Boujeloud. Although the style of the decorations is classic "Mauresque", the gate

31

dates from the beginning of the 20th century. Glazed tiles in the most intricate patterns decorate the upper part. Below is a ceremonial portal fit for a sultan on camelback, flanked by smaller, thinner horseshoe-arched gates for pedestrians.

### Bou Inania Medersa

Workmanship from the 14th century Merenid dynasty makes the Bou Inania Medersa of Fez one of the country's outstanding monuments. The religious school is divided from a prayer room by a refreshing stream of water channelled into the marble paving of the courtyard. Some splendid wood-carving surrounds the courtyard, and there are more decorative delights in ceramic tile and stucco. Just across the street a remarkable medieval clock, no longer in working order, was designed to be the definitive judge of prayer times.

### Dar Batha Museum

A spacious garden, home base for a squadron of twittering birds, adds to the appeal of the 19th-century Dar Batha palace, now a museum of Moroccan arts and crafts. The exhibits range from 14th-century keys, locks and doors to Middle Atlas carpets so sumptuous that visitors would be crawling over them if they weren't hanging on the walls. Notices in Arabic and French identify and explain traditional musical instruments, costumes, copper- and brass-work, 16th-century ceramics, ancient books and manuscripts.

### Karaouine Mosque

Until the construction of the Hassan II Mosque in Casablanca, the Karaouine Mosque of Fez was the biggest religious structure in Morocco. Founded in the 9th century and expanded in the 10th and 12th centuries, it is

---

**3 THE THREE BEST MUSEUMS** Highlights from Roman Morocco are assembled at the small but definitive **Archaeological Museum** in Rabat, noted for two exquisite bronze busts from Volubilis. Some Volubilis mosaics turn up at **Dar el Makhzen,** the museum of Moroccan arts in Tangier, also featuring masterpieces of folk art. In Fez, a 19th-century palace, **Dar Batha,** is now a showplace for Moroccan arts and crafts—treasures ranging from calligraphy to carpets.

surrounded on all sides by the throbbing medina. If you walk in a great circle you will eventually pass each of its 14 doors, each giving the most partial view, but you'll never see all of it. Inside is a 16-aisle prayer hall large enough for 20,000 of the faithful.

### Moulay Idris Zaouia

You might suddenly think you were in a church, but the candles and incense on sale just outside the door of the *zaouia* of Moulay Idris are part of a distinctive Islamic cult. Moulay Idris II, who made Fez a great 9th-century city, is buried here. You can see into the edge of the sanctuary, where women pass offerings through a hatch to the tomb of the sultan, considered a saint. This is as close as non-Muslims can get to the blessings thought to be available here.

### New Town

Fes el Djedid means "Fez the New", but it's not to be confused with the Ville Nouvelle of the French era. Fes el Djedid dates from the 13th century, when the Merenid sultan built a walled precinct of gardens, palaces, forts and, oddly, the Mellah, the Jewish ghetto.

The Ville Nouvelle, with broad avenues, is the centre of commerce, and here the populace congregates for the early evening promenade, punctuated by mint tea at outdoor cafés.

# MARRAKESH

As fabulous as its reputation, Marrakesh is a kaleidoscope of palm-lined boulevards ennobling the new town; ochre walls of clay, stones and straw enclosing the old; plus palaces, gardens, mosques, a seething marketplace, and, by way of background, the snow-capped High Atlas mountains.

Marrakesh was founded nearly a thousand years ago under the Almoravid dynasty. Destruction and elaborate rebuilding followed under the 12th-century Almohads, who can take credit for the Koutoubia Mosque and its landmark minaret. The 20th-century French are responsible for the spacious elegance of the Ville Nouvelle.

### Djemaa el Fna

The high-toned historical monuments can come later. First, sample contemporary life in North Africa's most colourful marketplace—but mind the pick-

# MARRAKESH

Souk el Khémis

Oued Issil

Av. Yacoub el Mansour

Cimetière musulman

Route des Remparts

Zaouïa de Sidi Bel Abbès

Bâb el Khémis

Bâb Tarhzout

Gare routière

Zaouïa de Sidi Ben Slimane

Cimetière musulman

Rue el Gza

**MÉDINA**

Bâb Debbarh

Bâb Doukkala

R. el Hart

Quartier

Bâb Debbarh

R. Fatima Zohra

Rue Riad el Arouss

Rue de Bâb Doukkala

Mosquée Ben Youssef

Médersa Ben Youssef

des Tanneurs

Mosquée de Bâb Doukkala

Dar el Glaoui

Koubba el Ba'adiyn

Zaouïa de Sidi Ben Salah

Bâb Aïlen

**SOUKS**

Rue de Bâb Aïlen

Rue Sidi Youb

R. Sidi el Yamani

Mosquée Mouassin

Rahba Kédima

R. el Ksour

Rue Sidi Boulabada

Rue Bâb Ahmad

Rue Farrane

Avenue Mohammed V

Piscine

Place de Bâb Ftouh

Rue Dabachi

Rue Douar Graoua

R. el Koutoubia

Place Jemaa el Fna

Dar Si Saïd (Musée des Arts marocains)

Bâb Ahmad

R. Moulay Ismaïl

R. Riad ez Zitoun el Kédim

R. Riad ez Zitoun el Jédid

Rue de la Bahïa

Palais de la Bahïa

Rue Imam el Rhezali

Mosquée de la Koutoubia

Av. Houmman el Fetouaki

R. Sidi Mimoun

R. de Bab Aguenaou

Av. Houmman el Fetouak

Pl. des Ferblantiers

Cimetière juif

Cimetière musulman

Boulevard el Yarmouk

Mosquée el Mansour

**MELLAH**

Bâb Aguenaou

Tombeaux saadiens

Palais el Badi

Rue Berrima

Bâb er Rob

Rue de la Kasbah

Dar el Makhzen (Palais Royal)

Bâb Ahmar

R. de Bâb Ahmar

Cimetière musulman

Méchouar

**N**

600 m

600 yd

Bâb Ksiba

R. du Méchouar

Jardin de l'Agdal

pockets. Djemaa el Fna is a non-stop circus in a square, with acrobats, jugglers, story-tellers, fire-eaters, snake-charmers, fortune-tellers, whirling dervishes, musicians, minstrels and wily salesmen offering magic potions for health and youth. Simultaneously, you can shop, eat, hire a scribe, have your hair cut or a tooth pulled. It's a dream of an open-air show, and although the tourists love it they make up only a small minority of the crowds, for this is where all of Marrakesh converges—day and night.

### The Souks

North of Djemaa el Fna Square, as you wander the maze of the souks, watch the craftsmen of Marrakesh at work. You'll probably have more contact with the middle-men who stock their wares and sometimes importune the tourists. All manner of necessities and trifles are on sale in the sprawl of covered streets and alleys—pottery, leather ware, wrought iron, clothing, cosmetics and the most bizarre "health foods". As is the custom, each speciality has its little neighbourhood, so you don't have to go far

*Bird man of Marrakesh follows a shopper, veiled to the spectacles, in the wool department of the souks.*

to compare the prices of a kaftan or a carpet. Among the sandal-makers you'll discover that those soft-leather pointed slippers *(babouches)* are made with the heel already tucked in. They're designed to slip on and off, as when visiting a mosque.

### Ben Youssef Medersa

In the centre of the medieval medina, you can visit a religious school founded in the 14th century, ornately refurbished much later under the influence of the Andalusian style. The splendid central courtyard of Ben Youssef Medersa is arcaded on two sides. You can go upstairs and visit what were the students' rooms, varying from the most monkish cells to rather grand rooms with a view. (For reasons of fair play the room assignments were rotated every Friday.)

### Koutoubia Mosque

Marrakesh is flat, conducive to seeing the sights by bicycle or *calèche,* horse and carriage. It's so flat that from almost anywhere in town you can see the landmark minaret of the Koutoubia Mosque, one of the three most beautiful minarets of the Almohad era (the others are in Rabat and Seville). Credit for its completion goes to Yacoub el Mansour, the sultan who stretched the realm to all of North Africa and 37 much of Spain. With many of its noble decorative details faded or missing, the graceful tower is under renovation.

### El Bahia Palace

Only a century old, this was the gardened residence of a grand vizier who enjoyed his autocratic power. Ornamentation in traditional designs is splashed everywhere in spare-no-expense style. Guides gleefully point out the living quarters of his four wives and countless girlfriends in the harem section, where, for security reasons, only blind musicians entertained and eunuchs served the tea.

### Dar Si Saïd Museum

This cool palace was built by a half-brother of the ambitious grand vizier responsible for the larger Palais El Bahia, nearby. It now houses a museum of Moroccan Arts. Specialities are Berber artefacts, historic and modern, from the south of Morocco—jewellery, costumes, pottery, carpets, furniture, toys and weapons.

### Saadian Tombs

The elegant 16th-century necropolis of the rulers of the Saadian dynasty was forgotten until the 20th century. Sultan Moulay Ismaïl, who spared no effort to efface the memory of his predecessors, had it walled up. Exquisitely carved Carrara marble is used unsparingly; in those days Moroccan sugar was traded for an equal weight of the finest imported marble. Under vaulted ceilings reminiscent of Andalusian palaces, the most handsome architectural detail is the *mihrab* (prayer niche) in the first mausoleum you see. Indoors and out, here are the tombs of sultans, princes, officials and servants. The most impressive of all

**4  THE FOUR MOST BEAUTIFUL GATES** Some say the vast 18th-century **Bab Mansour** in Meknès is the most magnificent gate in Morocco. A 20th-century competitor is the brightly decorated **Bab Boujeloud** in Fez. Impressive is the massive but delicately decorated 12th-century gate to the **Oudaïa Kasbah** in Rabat. And the oldest gate in Marrakesh, **Bab Agnaou,** has lovely designs and Kufic calligraphy cut in local stone.

belongs to Ahmad al-Mansur, the Saadian who took his troops to Timbuktu, assuring the profitable desert trade in gold and slaves.

### Agdal Garden

Begun in the 12th century, the Agdal Garden was expanded by the Saadians and now covers some 400 hectares (nearly 1000 acres). Hidden from sight within walls are citrus and olive groves, irrigated by a complex of channels that originate as far away as the Atlas mountains. The lake-sized pool at the centre of the irrigation system was used for royal boating excursions. Nowadays, considerations of hygiene rule out swimming.

### Menara Garden

Ancient olive trees and a historic pool distinguish the Menara Garden, west of the Agdal. The rectangular pool is filled with water from the mountains. Overlooking it all is a mysterious 19th-century pavilion. Just beyond the calm and beauty of the garden is a factory, which, the locals claim, cans Morocco's tastiest olives and purest olive oil.

### Oasis

Olive trees flourish on the south side of Marrakesh; on the north side it's palm trees. In a most scenic area, an estimated 180,000 palms provide shady paths and,

---

**SPEECHLESS**

You don't have to know the language. In any Marrakesh café the sound of jingling coins signals the arrival of the cigarette man—a furtive character selling them one by one to clients caught short, or unable to afford a full packet. The shoe-shine boy announces his trade by tapping his box of polish with his shoe brush. In the street beyond, most car horns sound gentle warnings to straying pedestrians, though traffic jams can inspire prolonged choruses of frustration.

---

much more practically, a supply of wood and fronds. Luxury villa and resort development has now bitten significantly into the palm grove, but it's still worth a visit. Especially if you're heading no farther south, in which case this may be your only chance to experience something of the atmosphere of an oasis.

### On the Slopes

Gazing up from the palmy Marrakesh skyline to the snow on the High Atlas mountains, thoughts turn to poetry or art—or winter sports. Skiing is the business of Oukaïmeden, Morocco's prime winter resort, south of Marrakesh. The ski-lifts go up to 3,268 m (10,722 ft).

# RESORTS
El Jadida, Essaouira, Agadir, Tafraoute, Taroudant

The best parts of the Atlantic coast south of Casablanca were colonized by the 16th-century Portuguese empire. The result is a mixed bag of ports, forts and villages with a charmingly skewed, foreign aspect. Linking them, the coastal highway offers dramatic vistas and access to an infinity of beaches.

## El Jadida

The intrepid ancient Phoenicians were here first. The Portuguese started all over again, called the port Mazagan, fortified it and held it against all foes for two and a half centuries. A spacious beach attracts swarms of Moroccan vacationers in summer.

El Jadida (meaning "New City"—renamed after the Portuguese left) has a remarkable Portuguese legacy in the ramparts and houses of the old city. Among the historic buildings inside the citadel are the governor's palace, a hospital, a prison, and a church later consecrated as a mosque. The most evocative place in town is the Cistern, an underground storage site four centuries old, in which 25 powerful pillars support the vaulted roof, reflected in the water on the floor.

## Safi

A city of around 200,000 people with fuming smokestacks, storage tanks and a fish-processing industry is not likely to be high on any tourist itinerary. But Safi is a natural refuelling stop if you're driving the coast road between El Jadida and Essaouira. Its harbour, the nearest port to Marrakesh, has been important for a couple of thousand years. All the industrial installations make the port about as inviting as a steel mill in summer, but history has left some worthwhile traces. The medina near the port was fortified by the Portuguese. A 16th-century fortress now houses the National Museum of Ceramics, concentrating on the work of local potteries, which still produce distinctive blue glazes.

## Essaouira

Until Moroccan independence, Essaouira was named Mogador. Its history goes back to Phoenician and Roman times, but the most visible influence is Portuguese: the Skala fortress is a classic 16th-century bastion recalling swashbuckling days. Some modern history: Orson Welles was lengthily based here filming *Othello*. Nowadays the excitement comes from legions of windsurfers who have spread the word internationally: the conditions along Essaouira's endless beach are perfect, and the relaxed town is a winner, too.

### The Port

Follow the gulls to the hardest-working fishing port you've ever seen, just beyond the fortifications. When the big trawlers come home, bucket brigades toss ashore baskets of fish from the ships' holds, to be laid out in trays and iced. Porters in rainwear and padded hats carry the dripping trays on their heads to waiting trucks. Meanwhile, crews prepare the ships and the nets for the next outing. It never stops. On the edge of the port, tempting fish and sea-food lunches are grilled *al fresco* for hungry locals and tourists.

For a panoramic view of all the excitement, climb to the top of the square bastion, the Skala, where you can also read the inscriptions on the collection of cannon from the 18th and early 19th centuries. There's a view of two rugged offshore islets, now a bird sanctuary.

### The Medina

A French architect, a captive of the sultan, designed Essaouira's unusual old walled town. His logical grid plan removes a lot of the mystery from the medina, though you can still get slightly lost in the back alleys. The souvenir shopping is good, and you might stumble on a hidden square where salesmen auction second-hand clothing, radios or junk. The sellers proceed around the square holding out their property for inspection and quoting a price, and often several rounds are needed before a buyer is found. The fish auction in the port is altogether more efficient and official.

## Agadir

More than 500 km (310 miles) southwest of Casablanca, Agadir is the place for sunny escapism: lazing on 10 km (6 miles) of soft, golden sand, riding a camel, windsurfing, parasailing, and deep-sea fishing for a shark or for dinner. The evenings bring difficult choices among the shops, the international restaurants, cafés and discos. All those assets and a new international airport make Agadir the number one tourist town in Morocco, the sort of resort where they have a menu printed in your language, no matter where you're from.

All that's missing is history. The clock stopped on leap day, February 29, 1960, when an earthquake more ruinous than its Richter rating destroyed the city. King Mohammed V mobilized the 41

*Supremely patient, a down-to-earth merchant awaits his first client.*

stricken nation: "If destiny desired the destruction of Agadir," he said, "its reconstruction depends on our faith and determination."

### The New City

Post-quake Agadir was built on seismically benign flatlands south of the zone of doom. The centre of the new city is a noisy hustle and bustle of concrete, commerce and traffic, but there are pedestrian malls and parks to relieve the urban stress, and an aviary called the Valley of the Birds. Beyond the business centre the city planners laid out industrial and residential zones. They re-

served the choicest real estate, paralleling the bay, for the hotel strip, where, as in Las Vegas, the newest hotel is usually bigger and more lavish than its neighbour. The tourist sector's expansion goes on for miles, with no end in sight. But, then, there's no end in sight for the glorious beach.

### The Kasbah

Discreet signs point the way to a winding road up to the top of a great hill where the ruins of the old town and the remains of thousands of earthquake victims lie within the walls of the old kasbah. The reinforced ochre ramparts are essentially all that's left. There's a gripping view out from the hilltop overlooking Agadir's port, the new city and the Atlantic, and camels are available for picture-posing. Inevitably, souvenir vendors hustle here, immune to the melancholy history of the site.

---

**AERIAL GOATS**

Like a Marc Chagall fantasy, goats "live it up" in the branches of trees along the roadsides near Agadir. As amazed tourists drive past, smiling goatherds proudly point to the agility of their charges. The climbing goats are not nearly so special as the trees, which are arganes, prospering only in this small area of Morocco. Arganes are rich in oil-rich nutty fruit—that's what the gourmet goats are after—and the wood itself makes excellent fuel.

---

The highly developed, modern port of Agadir is worth a visit (but take your passport). Big-time fish auctions are scheduled twice daily, in the morning and afternoon, and there are good fish restaurants, as well as informal outdoor grills.

## Tafraoute

Excursions from Agadir cut through mountain landscapes into the Ameln Valley, or Valley of Almonds, its charming villages and its main town, Tafraoute. The time to go is February, when the almond orchards are in blossom. Tafraoute itself adjoins a palm grove, with surreal granite outcrops just above, and the Anti-Atlas in the distance.

## Taroudant

The red walls encircling Taroudant are big and powerful enough to protect a metropolis, but everything within is low-slung and village-like. There are only two

---

**5 THE FIVE BEST BEACHES** Secluded coves and great sandy expanses, here are five of Morocco's best beaches, in counter-clockwise order from the Mediterranean to the Atlantic. **Al Hoceïma,** "pearl of the Mediterranean", backed by the Rif mountains; **Mohammedia,** a favourite of nearby Casablanca; **El Jadida,** ever-lively Atlantic resort; **Oualidia,** small family resort; **Agadir,** giant, gently sloping, sunny beach.

*Boxy red houses stare out at the world from a village near Tafraoute.*

main squares, between which you can get your bearings. A practical means of transport is the *calèche,* a horse-drawn carriage—and it's not just for tourists.

The crenellated city walls are pierced by five gates. Long before it was fortified, Taroudant was the ancient capital of the fertile Souss plain, with its olive and citrus orchards. After many ups and downs, going back to the 11th century, good times came in the 16th century under the Saadian dynasty, which made Taroudant its capital before choosing Marrakesh. The Alaouite sultan Moulay Ismaïl punished the town in 1687, wiping out

most of the citizens and their homes. The walls were restored but Taroudant never reached its earlier prominence again.

### The Souks

No great historical or architectural monuments grace Taroudant, but just roaming around the old town is a pleasure. Tourists being much less numerous than in Agadir or Marrakesh, the salesmanship is relatively low-key. The local "bargains" include antique jewellery and weapons (antiquity sometimes simulated), stone carvings, carpets, and handicrafts in general. The souks are varied and rich in local colour.

# The Moroccan Oases

## Illusion and Reality

A cool, green island hidden in the heart of the immense desert; a sanctuary that weary travellers yearn for; the paradise of Allah: the very word "oasis" has always conjured up the postcard image of a haven of peace and tranquillity. Camels may also come to mind, but chameleon is the apt word for the ever-changing desert: rocky here and sandy there, blazing hot by day and cold at night, fearsome on one side, poetic on the other. Just looking at the way a few splotches of grey scrub struggle to survive may make you feel thirsty—and heighten the delight when you sight an oasis. The camels, of course, are one-humped dromedaries.

## The Heyday of the Oases

Their roots go back to ancient times, but it was in the Middle Ages that the Saharan oases knew their days of glory. With the development of trade in Europe, and the establishment of commercial routes between Europe and black Africa, the oasis was not only a vital resting place for the desert caravans but also a supply post where provisions could be loaded. Setting out from Gao or Timbuktu, the seemingly endless caravans numbered thousands of camels laden with salt, and especially gold. These goods enabled the merchants around the western Mediterranean coast to purchase yet more valuable commodities, such as spices from the Orient or even further afield.

At the same time, the oases became important agricultural centres. In order to exploit this lucrative business, huge engineering projects, especially in irrigation, were undertaken in Morocco from the end of the 8th century, under the Merinids. Great wealth passed through the oases of North Africa, and it was not uncommon for an oasis such as the Tafilalt, to the east of Marrakesh, to number up to 100,000 inhabitants living in several hundreds of fortified villages.

## The Decline

After the 16th century, the discovery of the New World, and the promise of treasures it held in store, sounded the death-knell for trans-Saharan trade and the great caravans of the nomadic peoples. Europe was no longer interested in African gold, hitherto so coveted. They preferred 45

American gold, discovered in quantity and outrageously exploited by the Spaniards. The importance and splendour of the Saharan oases began to decline.

Despite the unhappy reality, the wonderful image of a rich patch of greenery in the midst of an adverse environment long remained fixed in the European consciousness. This was the era of the romantic novel, transporting whole generations in their imagination to the golden, sandy wastes. For the better part of a century, from the end of the 19th to the middle of the 20th, the oasis was something of a mirage.

Perhaps even more than the purple prose of popular literature, the lack of knowledge of the Sahara's realities contributed towards sustaining the myth. Until the early 1950s, the desert was scarcely more than a large blank space on the map. Little explored and largely ignored, the desert was left to itself. The general public only became aware of its existence with the discovery of oil. They then began to hear about oases where the populations were often living in conditions of extreme hardship. The disappearance of the caravans and the evolution of society had engendered great changes in the economic and social life of the oases. As in rural areas the world over, many of the young people had left to seek their fortunes in the towns. At the same time, agricultural activity was completely disrupted by the opening of new markets and the appearance of new production methods. The oases opened up to the outside world, with all the consequences that implied.

**The Oasis Today**

Nowadays, depending on the region, the situation has changed. In Morocco, an agricultural tradition persists: flourishing in the rich palm-groves of Tinerhir at the gateway to the Todra Gorge; much less prosperous in many of the southern oases. But rich or poor, they all have one feature in common: the caravans of yesterday have been replaced by coachloads of tourists.

**What is an Oasis?**

The gentle murmur of water bubbling from the spring and flowing along the irrigation canals, the pleasant coolness of gardens where vegetables and cereals grow, the green plumes of majestic palm trees: such is the magic of an oasis. At first glance they may all seem to follow the same pattern; in fact you'll soon discern their individual character.

*Ait Arbi kasbah in the Dadès Valley.*

47

## From Mountain to Desert

Initially, all oases were formed by a clump of vegetation that sprouted spontaneously. They are strung like beads along dry desert valleys, or encircle the base of arid mountains, wherever underground water comes close to the surface. *Wadis* are intermittent streams that well up only after heavy rain, but they often have a hidden subterranean flow. Some oases can stretch over several tens of miles, like the Tafilalt oasis in the region of Erfoud, or the Drâa Valley, a wadi south of Ouarzazate.

In Morocco, the "mountain oases" are more numerous. They are mostly found on the high plateaux along the foothills of the Atlas, carving gorges and valleys from the red and brown rock. The isolated "desert oases" are mainly scattered in the south and along the Algerian border.

## The Source of Life

Whatever their setting, all oases owe their existence to the presence of water. Whether it has collected underground or on the surface, or flows in the wadis rushing down from the mountains, it is essential. The hostile desert environment could not have been exploited without it.

The water is divided into three main categories. Spring and well water is reserved for human consumption; collected in ponds it is used for bathing, washing clothes and for watering livestock; the rest irrigates the crops. Traditionally, large, clay-lined holding basins serve as reservoirs. Main channels, *séguias,* lead from these basins and are further divided into secondary channels called *masraf*, carrying the water out to the smallest cultivated plot. An ingenious underground drainage system, the *khettara*, completes the installation.

Paradoxically, there's no lack of water in the desert. The only difficulty is bringing it to the surface. Already in medieval times, gigantic engineering projects were undertaken in the Moroccan oases to draw up water to irrigate the land. It was then that agricultural production began to develop, eventually transforming the oases into veritable larders.

## Lord of the Oasis

Another common feature of all the oases is the palm tree. Of the many crops to be found there, the date palm, *Phoenix dactylifera*, best symbolizes the oasis—with good reason. It flourishes beside patches of ground water or on the

*Wading in the wadi of the Todra Gorge.*

river banks, a noble tree with its feet in the water and its head in the sun. It has been cultivated and prized as the staple food and chief source of wealth in the oases since the remotest antiquity. Hanging from its branches are great clusters of "fingers of light"—*deglet nour,* the golden dates now widely exported and which for generations have provided a highly energetic food for local populations. More than half the weight of the dried fruit is sugar.

Every part of the palm is valuable: the trunk provides timber to build houses; the midribs of the leaves are handy for fencing; the leaves themselves are used for basket-weaving; the leaf bases and fruit stalks are for fuel, and even the date stones are used to feed the camels. Robust, the date palm is highly productive when properly managed, yielding up to 15 tons of dates per hectare per year. Especially in the south, the palm has displaced other less profitable or more delicate crops, transforming ancient gardens into immense palm groves of up to 35,000 trees, as at Tagmoute near Tata.

In the heart of the most beautiful oases, you will also discover a jungle of vegetation and a profusion of fresh vegetables. Carrots, turnips, lentils, watermelons, tomatoes and other crops grow in rotation all year round, among terraces of olives, figs, almonds, peaches, apricots and other fruit trees. To complete the picture, plantations of wheat, maize and cereals make a pleasing patchwork of colour.

## Kasbah and Ksour

The dwellings are generally grouped together in a higher, drier zone, so as not to waste the smallest strip of fertile land and to better protect the crops from human depredation.

The oasis is a fragile environment. The springs dry up after periods of drought; the wells are choked if a sandstorm blows, burying the palms beneath the dunes… In order to shelter from the elements, but mainly to protect themselves against invaders, the local populations reinforced their villages and homes. Their fortified villages are called *ksour* (singular: *ksar*). For further protection, wealthy warlords set up imposing strongholds, *kasbahs.* Built of mud on stone foundations, these are mainly found in the south and along the banks of the Drâa and the Dadès. There is no danger of attack nowadays, but the oasis dwellers continue to live like their ancestors in houses of *pisé*—a combination of clay, stone and straw—with hardly a concession to modernity. When you walk into one of

*Surrounded by palm groves, Tinerhir is the gateway to the Todra Gorge.*

these villages and savour its particular atmosphere, you might easily believe you have stepped back in time.

### Surviving the Desert

If you travel independently, then you should take one or two sensible precautions. Make sure that your vehicle is in good condition. As petrol stations are few and far between, top up the tank whenever you can, even if it is half full. Make sure you have a sufficient supply of water, and remember to drink frequently. Do not set out on a difficult journey without appropriate equipment, and obtain as much information as you can beforehand. Do not drive at night; it is always dangerous. During the day, drive carefully, watch out for other vehicles, pedestrians and animals, and pay attention to the state of the road. If your vehicle breaks down, stay near it instead of wandering off for help.

Whether you're driving, travelling by bus or by camel, you must remember to protect yourself adequately from the heat. You will need a hat and sunglasses, a sweater for night time and high altitudes, and stout walking shoes. Your clothes should be lightweight, preferably in pale colours. 51

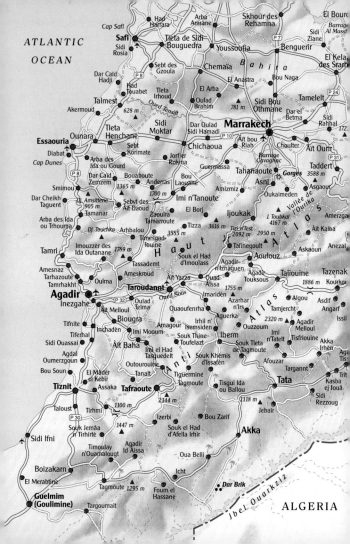

SOUTHERN MOROCCO:
DESERT AND OASES

# TO THE DESERT

Erfoud and the Eastern Oases, Dadès Valley,
To Zagora and the Southern Oases,
The Tata Circuit

Morocco's oases are located on the lower foothills of the Atlas Mountains and beyond, at the edge of the Sahara, along a line drawn between Er Rachidia and Goulimine, to the east and south of Marrakesh.

The most frequently visited are those in the region of Erfoud in the east and to an even greater extent, those in the region of Zagora in the south. From Erfoud, you can explore the Tafilalt, the largest palm grove in Morocco, and from Zagora, the Drâa Valley, one of the country's finest natural sites. The remoter oases deep in the south near Tata, in Berber territory, offer less spectacular landscapes, but it is still worth making the effort to get there.

## Erfoud and the Eastern Oases

Except during the Date Festival, held every October, the town of Erfoud is unprepossessing. However, it is situated right in the heart of the Tafilalt, Morocco's most important oasis, where a succession of palm groves, cultivated fields and *ksour* stretch more than 100 km (60 miles) north to the crossroads town of Er Rachidia. All around are great outcrops of black rocks crammed with fossils that children sell for a few *dirhams* by the road or at stopover points. Er Rachidia used to be known as Ksar es Souk when it was a French Foreign Legion fort. It is a strategic base for several excursions.

### Meski

A little to the south of Er Rachidia, the palm grove at Meski is irrigated by the Blue Springs, a natural groundwater pool named for the "Blue Men" of the desert, the Tuareg, for whom Meski was an obligatory halt. (Tuareg men veil their faces day and night—the women never—with a length of indigo-dyed cotton.) Beyond, one *ksar* after another follows the course of the Ziz river until it runs out on the edge of the desert.

Meski still makes a welcome and refreshing stop for those on their way to Erfoud and the Tafilalt.

*The family jewels, and more, add to the allure of a young villager from the High Atlas.*

### Rissani

For centuries Rissani, the capital of the Tafilalt region, was the last flicker of civilization for the southbound caravans. It was here that cargoes of metals, fabrics, dates and especially salt, were loaded onto the camels. Called the cradle of the Alaouite dynasty, this weatherbeaten village is where the ancestors of the present king established their religious power before triumphing in the 17th century. Nowadays, there's scarcely a trace of that prosperous era when more than 100,000 people, spread out in 600 settlements, lived here, and it takes a fertile imagination to conjure up an idea of its former glory. However, if you follow the rutted road that loops around Rissani, you will discover sleepy villages with winding lanes of baked-clay dwellings, huddled together in the suffocating heat. Here the landscape is fairly flat; the desert is on the doorstep. The further you venture, the more the desert encroaches, finally engulfing the last palm trees and receding crops.

### Erg Chebbi

You'll need four-wheel drive to make the detour to the dunes. Erg Chebbi, near the village of Merzouga, is the biggest sand dune in the country. It rises as high as 150 m (nearly 500 ft) and goes on for miles. It's a great place to be at daybreak. Camel rides into the scorching desert can be arranged from here, or you can just take a tentative hike in the sand.

### Jorf

If you travel from the Tafilalt to Ouarzazate, your route may pass through Jorf. There again, the landscape features a succession of ksour and palm groves. But beyond Jorf, you'll notice on each side of the road hundreds of little craters, a meter or so high. They are in fact wells, channelling deep beneath the earth to reach ground water collected a great distance away.

## Dadès Valley

The 300 km (190 miles) of tarred road leading from the Tafilalt to Ouarzazate, through the Dadès Valley, offer the opportunity to see a series of natural sites which are among the most impressive Morocco has to offer. Confined between the High Atlas and the Anti-Atlas ranges, the Dadès Valley contrasts the most arid scenery and heartlifting oases. Along the way are kasbahs, ksour and palm groves.

### Tinerhir and the Gorges

The modern regional centre of Tinerhir, bordering an oasis, is the gateway to the Todra Gorge. On the way into the mountains,

*With its brightly painted buildings, Rissani is a picturesque little village.*

the roadside villages, some in ruins, are as colourful as the cliffs.

At an altitude of over 1,000 m (3,300 ft), Tinerhir's palm grove stretches to the foothills of the Atlas mountains. The view is extraordinary, and it's worth spending an hour or two (before the sun gets too hot) observing the daily life of the people at work around the irrigation channels, in the orchards and the fields. This oasis is without question one of the most beautiful and most prosperous in the country.

The road into the Dadès Gorge (from Boumalne-du-Dadès) cuts through high cliffs of ever more striking colours. When it's dry, intrepid travellers go up and over the Atlas mountains from the Todra Gorge directly to the Dadès Gorge.

### Skoura

Around Skoura, you'll encounter a surprising outburst of roadside roses. The petals are converted into rosewater in a factory at El Kalaâ des M'Gouna, a fortified village where a rose festival is held every April.

Skoura's oasis has some remarkable *pisé* buildings standing against a glorious backdrop formed by the snowy peaks of the Great Atlas. Take care if you 57 wander into the palm grove at the edge of the town; it's easy to lose your way in this labyrinth of vegetation.

### Southern Route

An ancient piste, now tarred, links Erfoud to Zagora and the oases of the far south on the brink of the desert. You have to cross over interminable, monotonous, rocky plateaux, oppressed by a leaden sun, and you're likely to meet more camels than fellow-drivers. For the whole 250 km (160 miles), the only reprieve is provided by the oases of Alnif, with a pleasant palm grove, and Tazzarine, a welcome shady spot.

## To Zagora and the Southern Oases

If you come from the direction of Marrakesh, you'll see the majestic Drâa Valley appearing on the horizon once you have crossed the majestic High Atlas mountains at the pass of Tizi n'Tichka, at more than 2,200 m (7,200 ft).

### Ouarzazate

The gateway to the desert is an old French garrison town straggling along a wide main street 5 km (3 miles) long. Now Ouarzazate is a Moroccan army town with soldiers on bicycles trundling past the carpet salesmen. Local luxury hotels cater not only to coachloads of tourists anticipating their safaris but also to international film crews. Somewhere in Ouarzazate you're almost bound to bump into a recognizable movie actor or at least a temperamental cameraman. It all started in the 1960s with *Lawrence of Arabia*. The area is so well endowed in sunshine, dunes, camels and low-budget extras that the cameras of several nations have never stopped grinding out their epics here.

### Kasbah Taorirt

Ouarzazate's principal historical monument, at the crest of Avenue Mohammed V, is a kasbah, or feudal family castle. Kasbah Taorirt was built by the Glaoui warlords, who ruled by wile and force of arms over much of southern Morocco in the 19th century and well into the 20th. In its heyday the kasbah housed many relatives of the chiefs as well as an army of hangers-on, servants and craftsmen. Guides lead visitors through restored parts of the complex, most enthusiastically the former wives' quarters, recalling anecdotes of life in the harem. The traditional construction techniques, using palm wood, straw and mud, are readily visible.

From the upper storeys there's a view of the modern El Mansour dam that provides water and elec-

### MONDAY IN TINZOULINE

The village of Tinzouline, half-way between Agdz and Zagora, features a lively regional market on Mondays. In season there's a vast trade in dates, packed in standard boxes, which are transferred from grower to wholesaler almost before you know what's happening. An itinerant blacksmith forges shoes for mules brought to the village for the occasion. Sensitive visitors should keep their distance from the working abattoir in the midst of the market.

tricity for the district. The lake created by the dam surrounds an island topped by a ruined kasbah, and provides an unexpected opportunity for swimming or rowing in the midst of a desolate red landscape.

### Fint

Scarcely 15 km (9 miles) from Ouarzazate, the Fint oasis can be reached only along a stony piste. After miles of rocky black hills, you suddenly emerge into a splash of green in the hollow of a gorge. The site has served as the location for several films, but the inhabitants still follow their old ways, deliberately refusing to allow their oasis to be invaded by modern shops or tourist trappings. If you venture along the winding paths of the palm grove, you'll discover a friendly, appealing people, living frugally from the fruit of their labour.

### Drâa Valley

The road southeastwards from Ouarzazate yields sensational scenery: from stony desert across mile-high mountains, into the Drâa Valley with its historic kasbahs and dreamy palm groves. Few people are seen except for goatherd children selling dates in little straw baskets and women enjoying the desert luxury of washing clothes in a stream.

The literal high-point of the journey is the Tizi n'Tinififft pass, alt. 1,660 m (5,446 ft). The first stop after the descent from the mountain, a dusty village called Agdz, has the sort of amenities you've been looking for: cafés, basic hotels, taxis and a cluster of shops displaying carpets and pottery.

From Agdz to Mhamid, the two ends of the Drâa Valley, the river runs for 200 km (125 miles), irrigating palm groves and crops before vanishing into the sands of the desert. All along the valley, oleanders, date palms and acacias mingle with the ochre shades of the earth. It is a splendid landscape, whose changing colours are seen at their best during the first and last hours of daylight. A sprinkling of mysterious kasbahs and ksour are set back from the road. The windblown *pisé* walls often have elaborately carved designs. Sometimes they look close, but desert distances are deceiving and they can really be several kilometres away. The settlements recall ancient times when the sedentary populations had to battle against plundering bands of nomads from the south, come to help themselves to some of the riches of this fertile province.

### Zagora

A jokey direction sign in the centre of town proclaims that Timbuktu is 52 days away, by camel. As you take the inevitable picture you'll probably be offered the services of so-called false guides, who pester tourists at every opportunity. If you want a "real" guide, your hotel or the tourist office can provide a legitimate, knowledgeable professional—much cheaper than the tricksters. They will also show you the shops where the much sought-after carpets from the Drâa Valley are for offered for sale side-by-side with those made by the Tuareg tribes.

The road doesn't quite run out in Zagora, but this is where four-wheel drive vehicles come into their own. Here, too, you can arrange excursions by camel. The camel caravans still navigate by the stars, which seem to shine more brightly here in the desert. Even if you never sink into a dune, your first sunset in Zagora will confirm that the mystique is intact.

### Amazrou

The palm groves of Amazrou are a refreshing antidote to the stress of sightseeing. You can sip a cool drink or a hot mint tea and wait for the dates to fall from the trees, or you can do something strenuous like visiting the old Jewish kasbah. Most of the Jews of Amazrou, who made and traded silver jewellery, emigrated in 1958, but the synagogue still stands. Berbers have taken over some of the silver workshops.

### Tamegroute

This village is distinguished by a *zaouia*, or religious sanctuary, founded in the 17th century. The institution's Koranic Library, which may be visited, contains books and manuscripts up to nine centuries old. There are precious books on science and religion dating from Andalusia's golden age and venerable illuminated tracts of interest to visiting scholars.

### Mhamid

The paved road from Zagora finally runs out after 90 km (55

*In fertile Dadès Gorge, a kasbah is silhouetted against stark mountains.*

miles) in Mhamid. On the way, at Tinfou, are some small but evocative sand dunes. Amenable camels are available for photography sessions or brief excursions. Mhamid is the last oasis before the immense wastes of the Sahara. It is here, incidentally, where you are most likely to meet up with the "Blue Men", the Tuareg, who come on market days to exchange carpets and craftware for staples.

## The Tata Circuit

Well beyond Marrakesh and Agadir, and off the beaten track, the route to Tata and beyond reveals another side to Morocco, allowing contact with places and people which is arguably more authentic.

### Taliouine

Some 100 km (60 miles) east of Taroudant, Taliouine makes a good stopover for visitors heading south over the Anti-Atlas into Berber lands. This little village in the Djebel Sirwa area specializes in saffron, culled from the crocus plants growing in the gardens of the oasis. A cooperative on the edge of town sells the yellow spice at a very reasonable price. Not only for culinary purposes—it's also used as a colouring and an antispasmodic medicine.

### Tata

You have to cross the Anti-Atlas to reach Tata. The road climbs to 2,000 m (6,500 ft), through an untamed landscape of sparse vegetation and rocky canyons striped in many colours.

A few kilometres after the oasis of Tagmoute and its 35,000 palms, Tata heaves into view. The principal town of Tata province, with rose-coloured walls and arcaded streets, it has all the commodities a tourist may need. It stands in the middle of a lovely oasis watered by three wadis which rise in the Anti-Atlas. A palm grove and spring offer pleasant respite from the searing heat.

### Akka and Beyond

An old piste, now tarred, links Tata with Goulimine. There's very little traffic on this road, which crosses wide, emtpy plateaux open to the Sahara for 300 km (more than 185 miles). Whipped by a scorching wind, sand from the desert mingles with the rocks and stones of the Atlas, while here and there the first dunes appear.

The landscape could hardly be more arid and forbidding, but now and then you'll meet a flock of goats along the road, indicating the proximity of a village. Akka, with its low-profile houses and sandswept streets, is planted with date palms and various other fruit trees. You can wander beside the streams flowing through the palm grove, where you'll see the remains of the mellah, the old Jewish quarter, on the hillside.

After Akka, you pass several other oases, all on the old caravan route from the Sahara: Tisgui, Foum el-Hassan (known for its rock carvings), Icht and its fortified village, Tarhjiit, Tagmoute and finally Goulimine. Tuareg blue men still gather in Goulimine for the summer *moussem* (festival) and camel market. This last is also held on Saturdays, mainly for the benefit of day trippers. At other times, you may be the only foreigner, and you'll feel as though you're light years away from Marrakesh and the coastal resorts.

Amtoudi is the most famous of all the oases in the region—and the most visited, although it means a detour from the main road. An old kasbah watches over it from on high, renowned for its *agadir*, a medieval communal granary. Climb up for a stunning view of the gorges carved out in the bed of the wadi, sheltering a wide variety of fruit trees. Close to the palm grove, you can swim in a natural spring.

*On the road to the Tizi n'Tichka pass, the kasbah of Telouet.*

# CULTURAL NOTES

You'll feel right at home in hospitable Morocco—well, up to a certain point. Being in a country with a different religion, languages and customs is bound to test anyone's adaptability. Here are a few brief pointers toward understanding the culture of the country.

**Islam**. The word literally means "submission", as in "submission to the will of God", or Allah. The youngest of the world's principal religions, Islam is the official state religion of Morocco. At the beginning of the 7th century, the faith's founder, a merchant from Mecca named Mohammed, heard divine instructions and compiled the word of God in the Koran (meaning "recitation"). Before the century was out, the new religion came to Morocco. Hassan II, the present king, who traces his ancestry to the Prophet, is the spiritual as well as political leader of the nation.

**Obligations**. The Five Pillars of Islam affect every Moroccan's daily life. The creed must be recited: "There is no god but God, and Mohammed is his prophet." Prayers are scheduled five times daily, and communally in the mosque on Friday. A Muslim has to be charitable. During the holy month of Ramadan, strict rules of abstinence and piety must be respected. And everyone able to do so must make a pilgrimage to Mecca (in today's Saudi Arabia) at least once in a lifetime.

**Muezzin**. Five times a day, starting before dawn, the chant of the muezzin calls the faithful to prayer. In some countries the call is recorded and transmitted by loudspeaker, but in Morocco the voice from the heights of the minaret, even when electronically amplified, is "live". Other religions summon the faithful to services by horns or bells, but Mohammed himself is said to have found the human voice preferable for the purpose.

**Holidays**. The lunar calendar determines the dates of religious holidays, while the civic holidays follow the western calendar. Independence Day always falls on November 18, but Ramadan can be any time, even any season, depending on the moon's schedule. The holy month, a sort of Islamic Lent, requires fasting from sun-up to sunset, which is a tougher test on longer summer days than in winter. Nightfall brings feasting and rousing celebrations that more than compensate for the asceticism.

Incidentally, non-Muslims are not obliged to observe Ramadan's restrictions, but discretion is clearly advisable.

**Moussem**. Most of the hundreds of celebrations called *moussem* venerate local saints. Combining religious and social elements, they can be as simple as a glorified market day or as elaborate as a full-scale folklore festival, with music, dancing, feasting and *fantasias*, the spectacular displays of horsemanship. They happen in all parts of the country all the time but the best chance of stumbling on them occurs in August, September and October, when they double as harvest festivals.

**Hammam**. The institution goes back to the ancient Roman tradition, but it's also part of the Islamic requirement of cleanliness. Moroccans enjoy the relaxation of public baths, the hammam. When they are alongside mosques, hammams are ritual baths, and non-Muslims may not be welcome. Otherwise they are a gathering place, usually scheduled for men early in the morning and women later, though some hammams are permanently segregated. The piping hot steam baths are intended to alternate with cold-water relief. A massage and a nap round off the treatment.

**Art**. The Koran proscribes representations of living things, so Islamic art developed in abstract directions. Thus elaborate floral, geometric and calligraphic decorations embellish everything from the walls of mosques to ceramic tiles. The intricately intertwined flowers, leaves and geometrical motifs came to be called arabesque designs. The ban on figurative art is not total in Morocco. In art galleries and markets you'll see modern paintings of scenery, animals and even people—and some avant-garde abstractions, as well.

**Music**. You may be reminded of the wail of the Andalusian flamenco, but the music of Morocco is as varied as it is difficult for the outsider to digest. If the harmonies perplex, the rhythms are compelling. The instruments can be flutes, lutes, woodwinds, fiddles and tambourines, the voices sad or exalted. The influences are Berber, Arab, Jewish, Spanish and international. Relax and give it a try.

**Languages**. The North African version of spoken Arabic is a long way from classical Arabic or the language of, say, Egypt. Colloquial Berber is spoken by a strong minority of the population—in three dialects, depending on the region. French is very widely understood everywhere. In northern Morocco, for historical reasons, Spanish is the principal foreign language. English has growing impact in commercial and tourist circles, and in tourist areas German is ever more widely known.

# Shopping

*For shoppers visiting Morocco, the thrill of the hunt may be as much fun as the prize. In the mysterious, fragrant atmosphere of the souks you finally see what you want. Even if you don't meet the artisan who created the finest souvenir of your trip, you'll remember the shop or stall where you found it, and the charming salesman who convinced you this was just what you needed. Later, if hindsight shows you paid too much, regret nothing—just chalk it up to the educational or entertainment value of the experience.*

## Where to Shop

In the medina, you can watch the artisans hammering out copper trays, forging original jewellery and sewing kaftans with flashing needles. You can't shop any closer to the source. The trouble is knowing the price; haggling is required in the souks. For Moroccans, there's nothing underhanded abour haggling. It's a normal part of business, a way for buyer and seller to get to know each other and the real value of the product in question.

If this game intimidates or bores you, look for an *ensemble artisanal,* a government-sponsored shop featuring a wide variety of quality goods at fixed prices. At these centres you can see what's available, learn the going prices, and, if you're smitten, buy without pressure. Or return to the souks with renewed confidence in the value of things and haggle the day away.

## Carpets

Carpet weaving is the very oldest skill in the Moroccan repertory. The output is divided into two main categories: city and country carpets. The centres of production are Rabat, Meknès, Fez and Marrakesh. You may be able to visit a cooperative where girls aged 6 or 7, apprentices, weave the simple borders of rugs to be filled in by experts, following the complex diagrams of staff designers. More spontaneously, countrywomen create highly prized Berber carpets in the Atlas mountains and as far south as the Ouarzazate region. Keep your

*Hand-made carpet may lure you inside this shop in a Drâa Valley village.*

eyes peeled for carpets hanging out in villages and at weekly markets in off-beat towns. Irregularity in the design or shape is proof of authenticity.

## Costumes

It's hard to resist the urge to buy a burnoose or a fez or some other item of Moroccan clothing to show off to friends. At worst they can be useful at costume parties. The best bet is the kaftan, the all-encompassing woman's dress, which comes in luxuriously embroidered varieties—bound to elicit admiring reactions and interesting conversations when you're entertaining at home.

## Jewellery

Morocco's Jews were always the specialists in creating and selling jewellery, but most have emigrated; yet interesting jewellery can still be found. Gold is a favourite medium in the cities, silver in the villages and in the mountains. Silver alone or combined with amber turns up in necklaces, heavy brooches and wrist-, arm- and ankle-bracelets. Gold can be the setting for precious stones in rings, necklaces and earrings.

## Leather Goods

The leather of Morocco is so celebrated that the English language has linked the country and the 67 product since at least the 17th century. Precious books are morocco bound. The French were similarly impressed when they began to use the word *maroquinerie* to mean leather goods in general. The softest leather is used for everything from purses and desk sets to those comfortable Arabian-nights slippers called *babouches*. You'll also be offered leather luggage, wallets, belts, cushions and saddles. Fez and Marrakesh have the principal traditional tanneries.

## Metalwork

You'll hear them before you see them—artisans chipping away, decorating copper and brass plates, bowls or ashtrays, with geometric designs, swirls and arabesques. Wrought-iron experts produce kasbah-style lamps, grills, mirror frames and candlesticks. Or you can take home a tea-pot of silver or pewter to keep alive the memory of mint tea.

## Stones

In Taroudant the local limestone is worked into elaborately decorated candlesticks, boxes and paperweights. Along mountain roads, local children and more forceful adults reflect the sun into your eyes from rough pieces of quartz, amethyst and crystal they are selling. Prices vary enormously.

## Wickerwork

There's no end to the choice of wickerwork on sale all around the country—baskets, table mats, boxes, sun hats. The biggest variety is sold in the souks of Tetouan, Salé, Fez and Marrakesh.

## Woodwork

Aromatic cedar takes on a variety of forms, from chairs and inlaid boxes to figurines and chess sets. In Essaouira they are famous for working thuya, a multicoloured hardwood that comes to a high gloss. In Fez and Tetouan there are painted chests, boxes and cradles.

## Market Days

Some of the most animated weekly markets, at which tradesmen, artisans and country folk converge colourfully:

| | |
|---|---|
| Agadir: | Saturday and Sunday |
| Chaouen: | Thursday |
| Goulimine: | Saturday (camel market) |
| Marrakesh: | Thursday (camel market) |
| Ouarzazate: | Sunday |
| Rissani: | Sunday, Tuesday and Thursday |
| Taroudant: | Friday |
| Tiznit: | Thursday and Friday |
| Zagora: | Wednesday and Thursday |

# Dining Out

There's more to Moroccan cuisine than couscous. As varied as the country, the food can match any appetite, whether you're in the mood for subtle elegance or hearty peasant fare. The flavours are so subtle you'll have to sit back and analyze them. Beyond the native specialities, in any sizable city you'll find acceptable, often superior, French restaurants. In the north, Spanish cuisine gets special emphasis. If you crave a pizza or a hamburger, this sort of exotica, too, is close at hand.

## Breakfast

Some hotels lay on big buffets of hot and cold foods for breakfast—everything from cornflakes to fried eggs with a wide range of home-baked pastries. Other hotels serve a continental breakfast consisting of a croissant and a roll with butter and jam, and coffee, tea or hot chocolate. Whatever the offer, look for the local orange juice, which is wonderfully refreshing.

## Moroccan Specialities

Whether you're eating in a fancy restaurant or the most basic café deep in the medina, a great way to start a meal is *harira*, a chickpea soup that really "sticks to your ribs". Depending on the cook or the occasion, it may contain meat chunks, lentils, pumpkin, onions and tomatoes.

## Tajines

The name comes from the earthenware pot in which the *tajine* is stewed. The recipe can feature lamb, mutton, veal or beef, with a rich supporting cast of potatoes, tomatoes, onions, beans, olives, lemon and herbs and spices. There are fish *tajines*, as well.

Chicken stews come in lavish varieties—in unexpected alliance with olives and lemon or prunes and almonds. The chicken is cooked so slowly it all but removes itself from the bones.

## Couscous

North Africa's most famous dish takes a formidable amount of work to prepare authentically. The semolina has to be subdued into delicate, almost microscopic grains, none mingling in lumps, and steamed, flavoured and re-

steamed just so. Lamb, chicken or fish goes on top, with a spicy sauce and potatoes, chick-peas, peppers, tomatoes, courgettes, turnips, pumpkins and raisins.

## Pastilla

Flaky pastry fit for angels and infinite patience in the kitchen make Moroccan pigeon pie, called *pastilla,* or *bstilla,* a masterpiece. The pigeons are cooked first with onions and saffron, then the meat plus almonds and spices is interspersed with layers of pastry, coated with sugar, cinnamon and egg yolk. It all adds up to a sumptuous delicacy.

## Mechoui

In your travels you may stumble on a festival at which a whole lamb on a spit is being roasted over the coals. This is *mechoui,* a festive affair so good that it is reproduced at the most expensive tourist banquets. While the meat is being cooked and basted, the aroma sends out enticing signals to the appetite of anyone within range.

## Fish and Seafood

The best Atlantic and Mediterranean fish and seafood—from sardines to lobster—grace Moroccan restaurant tables, most commonly along the coasts. Specialist restaurants in the ports provide memorable grilled sea bass, mullet, tuna steaks, prawns, mussels and squid. Look over the day's catch, choose what looks right, then order some fish soup while the cooks go to work.

## Desserts

Sweets tend to be very sweet in Morocco, dripping with sugar or honey or both. For some sort of record in sweetness per cubic centimetre, try *dattes farcies,* dates stuffed with marzipan. If you find them too syrupy, there's always fresh fruit to vary the diet: melons, oranges, strawberries, bananas or peaches.

## Drinks

Many bars and restaurants in hotels and the *nouvelles villes* are licensed to serve beer, wine and spirits. During the French era, Morocco became a serious wine-producing country and there are very drinkable local vintages—red, white and rosé. Ask the waiter for advice. Locally brewed beer is popular, and cheaper than imported brands. The great majority of Moroccans respect Islam's view about alcoholic drinks. They devote themselves, instead, to round-the-clock consumption of sweet mint tea, as a look at any café terrace will reveal. At its best, with fresh mint floating in the pot, this is a most soothing drink to linger over, in any season.

# Sports

*Making the most of its diversified geography and climate, Morocco has something attractive for sports enthusiasts of every stripe, whether water-skiers or snow skiers. For just watching, the great national enthusiasm is football (soccer); Morocco is a world power in the sport.*

## On Sea

With a sea-and-ocean coastline long enough for any adventure, the country is inviting for water sports, starting with swimming and going on to windsurfing, sailing and deep-sea fishing.

**Surfing.** Those Atlantic waves have come all the way from the southeast coast of the United States, which is one reason international surfers find them challenging. Among popular hangouts are: Mehdia beach (near Kenitra), Plage des Nations (Rabat), Safi beach, Sidi Kaouki (near Essaouira), and many spots near Agadir—with suggestive names like *Rocher du Diable* (Devil's Rock) and "Banana".

**Sailing.** Yacht clubs are strung along the coasts all the way from Tangier to Agadir, with a concentration of activities in centres like Rabat and Casablanca. The Mohammedia Yacht Club runs international regattas every Sunday from May to October.

**Fishing.** Boat trips to rich fishing grounds can be arranged in the principal ports. Professionals in the resorts know when and where the big ones—blue fin tuna, swordfish, barracuda and friends—are waiting to be pulled in. Lake and river fishing for trout or pike is popular in the Middle Atlas. You have to get a permit from the *Direction des Eaux et Forêts,* headquartered in Rabat but with offices in all the cities.

## On Land

**Golf.** You're in good company on the links: King Hassan II is a dedicated golfer. The most grandiose golf complex in the country is the Royal Golf Dar-es-Salam, near Rabat, where Robert Trent Jones designed two 18-hole courses and a 9-hole bonus. Another prestigious place to play is the 18-hole links at Mohammedia. More golf is centred on Casablanca, Marrakesh, Tangier, Meknès, Fez and Agadir.

*On Morocco's Mediterranean coast: sandy beaches and smooth sailing.*

**Riding.** Equestrian clubs are scattered around the country in towns and resorts. Some of the luxury hotels have their own stables for the convenience of their guests. Increasingly popular are organized treks into the Middle Atlas, lasting one day or several.

**Hunting.** *Réserve Touristique d'Arbaoua,* is a happy hunting ground among foreign tourists. Located near Larache, in northwestern Morocco, it's available only to non-residents. The marshy plateau is rich in wild boar and bird life, both resident and transient. You have to show a hunting licence from your home country to get a temporary Moroccan licence.

**Skiing.** From Fez, Meknès and Marrakesh, the ski slopes are within easy reach. The most highly developed ski resort in the High Atlas is the Oukaïmeden (altitude 2,600m—8,500 ft), at the end of a dependably snow-free road from Marrakesh. The season usually lasts from December to March. In the Middle Atlas, the most popular resort is Michliffen, near Ifrane, at 2,000 m (6,500 ft). The contrast between the heat of the imperial cities and the snow on the slopes is one of Morocco's delights.

73

# The Hard Facts

*On the countdown to your trip, here are a few essential points you ought to know about Morocco:*

## Airports

Most flights, domestic and international, converge on Casablanca's Mohammed V Airport. The impressive modern terminal contains a tourist office, car hire desks, currency exchange counters, shops, a post office, bars and restaurants, and a prayer hall. There are free luggage trolleys. The second busiest airport, Agadir, has non-stop flights to and from several European capitals. Marrakesh, Tangier and Ouarzazate are among other cities handling some international traffic. Royal Air Maroc domestic flights link towns all the way to Laayoune and Ad'Dakhla in the extreme south.

## Car hire

International and local car hire companies compete for customers. You can sign up by the day with a supplement per kilometre driven, or for three days or a week with unlimited mileage included. The minimum age is 21, though some companies draw the line at 25. The easiest way to pay is with a credit card;

otherwise you will be required to put down a big cash deposit. Some companies let you pick up the car in one city and return it in another, at no extra cost.

## Climate

Most of the year temperatures are temperate in most of Morocco. Near the coast the influence of the sea moderates summer heatwaves, and in winter the average temperatures rarely drop below 10°C (50°F). The interior of the country, with a continental climate, is hotter than the coast in summer and colder in winter. It's three times rainier in Tangier than in Agadir. Desert summers are best avoided.

## Communications

Coin-operated and card-operated telephones are found in railway and bus stations, cafés and other public places. Direct-dial service covers the entire country. If you have enough coins, you can make an overseas call from a street-corner phone. In the post office (PTT) there is normally a separate wing handling telecommunications. Calling from your hotel room usually involves a surcharge, which can be substantial.

Mail works relatively efficiently. The PTT sells stamps, as do places that deal in postcards. For fastest processing of your homeward bound postcards, use the post box in the PTT.

## Complaints

If you think a fast-talking salesman in the souk has taken advantage of you, it's probably too late to have the price reduced. In all cases involving money, like hiring a guide or a horse-and-carriage—avoid the problem by settling on a price beforehand. Otherwise, most problems can be negotiated with a shrug and a smile. In a hotel or restaurant ask to see the manager.

## Currency

The unit of currency is the Moroccan *dirham* (DH), divided into 100 *centimes*. In practice, tourists rarely see anything smaller than a half-dirham coin. Coins go up to 5 DH. Banknotes are issued in denominations of 10, 50, 100 and 200 DH.

Well-known credit cards are accepted in hotels, restaurants and some shops. It's best to change traveller's cheques at the bank. Eurocheques are also useful at banks and in some shops

and hotels. Always have your passport with you as identification when changing money.

## Driving

The roads are generally good, and there is even an expressway (toll road) between Casablanca and Rabat. But the local standard of driving—and walking, too—means you can never relax your vigilance.

The regulations resemble those of France; direction signs are normally written in French as well as Arabic. Other than the unpredictable human element, such as country folk and livestock meandering down the middle of a highway, the dangers include the weather. Tracks *(pistes)* in mountain and desert regions can be flooded by melting snow or sudden rainstorms, and accumulations of snow can snarl the mountain roads between November and springtime.

Night driving in general can be very dangerous, with unlit bicycles, animals, potholes and other surprises potentially around every bend. Pleasant tree-shaded rest areas with picnic tables are frequently found along the highways; they are sign-posted *"Aire de repos"* well in advance.

In and around the towns there are plenty of petrol stations to choose from but be sure to fill up 75 before undertaking any wilderness jaunts. (Stations supplying lead-free petrol are rare but well signposted.) Speed limits are normally 40 km per hour in towns and 100 km per hour on the highway.

### Drugs

If you are offered *kif*, the highly regarded local hashish, be very prudent; some dealers are reputed to be police informers, and penalties can be stiff.

### Essentials

Just about anything you might need can be bought on the spot in Morocco, but if you require prescription drugs be sure to carry your own. A comprehensive first-aid kit is good to have, and don't forget insect repellent and sun-screen cream.

As for clothing, remember that nights are chilly in the desert and the mountains. For Morocco's conservative environment you'll need very modest styles; "revealing" fashions are okay in a resort hotel but not in a typical village.

### Formalities

For most tourists no visa is required to enter Morocco; all you need is a valid passport. If you are on a tour organized by a travel agency and hold a hotel voucher, your national identity card is sufficient. Note that if you look like a hippy you may be refused entry. You have to fill in a form for the immigration department on arrival. The Customs inspectors will probably wave you through.

For the record, you can bring into Morocco 200 cigarettes or 50 cigars and one litre each of wine and spirit. The only complication is money: it's forbidden to import or export the national currency, the *dirham*. But you can bring in as much foreign currency as you wish. Change it into dirhams a bit at a time, according to need. You are supposed to change all your dirhams into foreign currency before leaving the country. Shops in the departure area of the airport do not accept dirhams even if you are smuggling them.

### Health

No special inoculations are required for visiting Morocco. Consult your doctor in case he recommends topping up the shots you may have had for previous trips, especially if you'll be travelling in the south. A travel health insurance policy is a wise investment before you leave home. On the spot, avoid too much sun; start with morning and late afternoon outings, and splash on the sunscreen lotion. It's prudent to drink mineral water and avoid dubious food stalls. If the worst happens, any pharmacy will dole out pills to hurry you back to health. In case you need a doctor, the pharmacy, your hotel or your consulate can recommend one.

Water is generally fit to drink but to be on the safe side, especially in the south, stick to bottled mineral water or the national standby, mint tea.

## Holidays and festivals

Because two calendars are used in Morocco—the standard Gregorian model of 365 days as well as the Muslim year, which is 11 days shorter—things tend to be complicated. New Year's Day, a national holiday, always falls on January 1, but religious holidays follow a different rhythm. Consequently there's no such thing as a religious holiday that always occurs at a certain season.

Here is the line-up of non-religious public holidays:

| | |
|---|---|
| January 1 | New Year |
| March 3 | Fête du Trône (Coronation of King Hassan II) |
| May 1 | Labour Day |
| May 23 | National Day |
| July 9 | King's Birthday |
| August 14 | Allegiance Day |
| November 6 | Anniversary of the Green March |
| November 18 | Independence Day |

## Media

Moroccan dailies are published in Arabic, French and Spanish. British and European newspapers and the *International Herald Tribune* are sold at news kiosks in all the big cities.

In addition to Moroccan television, in Arabic and French, many hotels provide satellite service, relaying programmes from French, Italian, German and English-language networks.

## No entry

If you are non-Muslim you will not be allowed to enter the prayer halls of mosques in Morocco. However, you can get a peek into some of the most impressive ones. Among the few places excepted from the no-go rule are the Mohammed V mausoleum in Rabat and the sanctuary of Moulay Ismaïl in Meknès.

## Opening hours

Most administrative offices are open from 8.30 a.m. to noon and from 2.30 to 6.30 p.m., with a longer break on Fridays in deference to midday prayers.

Banks open Monday to Friday from 8.15 to 11.30 a.m. and again from 2.15 to 4 p.m. In summer, though, they operate nonstop from 8 a.m. to 3 p.m. And during the holy month of Ramadan the schedule is 9.30 a.m. to 2 p.m.

Main post offices are open from 8 a.m. to 6.30 p.m. Monday to Thursday; Fridays it's 8 a.m. to noon and 4 to 6.30 p.m. Summer hours are curtailed.

Shops in the medinas tend to operate from 8 a.m. to 9 p.m. daily, with a Friday break for prayers. In the *nouvelles villes,* a daily siesta from about noon to 3 p.m. is standard.

Museums follow an erratic schedule but most take a midday break.

### Photography

Well-known brands of film are sold in the cities and resorts, but the supplies may have been poorly protected against heat and light. Be prepared for wide variations in exposure, from the deep shadows of the kasbah to the blinding reflection of sun on white houses. You don't have to speak the language to ask someone's permission before taking a picture. Taking photos of women, in particular, can be a sensitive matter. Sensitive, too, are military installations, ports and airports, where photography is forbidden.

### Police

Municipal police, who direct traffic, will be helpful and courteous if you need directions. The Sûreté Nationale fights crime in towns and also patrols the highways. Another police organization, the Gendarmerie, deals with security and operates roadblocks in sensitive areas.

In much of the country, the telephone number for emergency police business is 19.

### Safety

Carrying whopping bankrolls or flashy jewellery only tempts fate. Keep valuables in your hotel safe. Leave nothing of value in a car, visible or hidden, locked or unlocked. In crowded markets and terminals beware of pickpockets.

### Social graces

Moroccans are friendly and open with visitors. Much hand-shaking goes on, but that's about as much formality as you're liable to meet. You shouldn't be too polite; for instance, a waiter might be offended to be called "sir" or thanked too effusively.

If you can learn a few elementary phrases in Arabic you'll be rewarded with surprised smiles and kindnesses.

### Taxis

*Petits taxis,* small cars with rooftop luggage racks, take up to three passengers on trips within cities (and up to 10 km or 6 miles beyond). Most have meters. For longer distances, or excursions, choose a more spacious *grand taxi,* but negotiate the price if it's an excursion.

## Time

All year round all of Morocco is on Greenwich Mean Time (GMT)—the same time as Britain in winter, one hour behind in summer.

## Tipping

People often let you know, subtly or otherwise, when a tip is appropriate. Don't forget waiters in cafés and restaurants, porters in hotels and terminals, toilet attendants, taxi drivers, helpful museum curators, and (not at all optional) those human parking meters, *gardiens de voitures.*

## Toilets

Your best bet is to "borrow" the facilities just off the foyer in any luxury hotel. There are also public conveniences in airports, rail stations, restaurants and cafés.

It's considered the minimum courtesy to invest in a mint tea or a drink if you're using the toilet in a café. Experienced travellers always carry their own toilet paper.

## Touts

In the tourist office in Fez, a sign warns: "Tourists: you may be approached by unauthorized guides offering tours of the city. These people are uncontrolled and we strongly advise you to avoid their services." The so-called "false guides", touts and hustlers are a problem in all the places that tourists congregate. Try to say "no" with a smile, and don't get flustered. If you're really lost, ask any child to lead you back to civilization.

The ministry of tourism takes hassling seriously and has advised that special "tourist squads" will be formed to act against street hustlers and illegal guides, and to assist foreign visitors in tourist areas such as Marrakesh, Fez, Meknès and Agadir.

## Transport

ONCF, l'Office National des Chemins de Fer, runs a comprehensive train service among most of the main Moroccan cities. The busiest line, between Casablanca and Rabat, has frequent, speedy trains, with the comfort level in 2nd class up to European standards. Air-conditioned luxury coaches roll along the highways between all the principal cities; regional buses are slower and less comfortable.

## Voltage

The standard is 220-volt A.C., with French-style plugs. But some towns are still on 110-volt power, so you'd better ask.

# INDEX

General editor: Barbara Ender-Jones
The Moroccan Oases: Michel Puysségur and Judith Farr
Layout: André Misteli
Photos: Hans Weber, Bernard Joliat, Michel Teuler, A.G.E. FotoStock,
Hémisphères/Wysocki
Maps: Elsner & Schichor, JPM Publications